Crossing the
Finish Line

Crossing the Finish Line

How to Retain and Graduate Your Students

Alan Seidman

ROWMAN & LITTLEFIELD
Lanham • Boulder • New York • London

Published by Rowman & Littlefield
An imprint of The Rowman & Littlefield Publishing Group, Inc.
4501 Forbes Boulevard, Suite 200, Lanham, Maryland 20706
www.rowman.com

Unit A, Whitacre Mews, 26-34 Stannary Street, London SE11 4AB

British Library Cataloguing in Publication Information Available

Library of Congress Cataloging-in-Publication Data Available

ISBN: 978-1-4758-3890-9 (cloth : alk. paper)
ISBN: 978-1-4758-3891-6 (pbk. : alk. paper)
ISBN: 978-1-4758-3892-3 (electronic)

To my wife, Barbara, for her continued support in my efforts to help college students achieve their academic and personal goals.

I also dedicate this to those colleges who are bold enough to implement the Seidman retention formula and model and prove that there is a way to help all students succeed.

Further, I dedicate this to the students who will benefit and complete their academic and personal goals based on my retention formula and model.

Contents

Preface

Seidman Says

Over the past thirty years of working on college student retention issues, I have coined some one-line sayings that sum up my thoughts on the topic. They are below.

- For intervention programs and services to be successful, they must be powerful enough to effect change (Seidman, 2005).
- $\text{Ret} = \text{Early}_{\text{ID}} + (\text{E} + \text{In} + \text{C})_{\text{IV}}$—that is, Retention = Early Identification + (Early + Intensive + Continuous) Intervention (Seidman, 2005).
- Retention is about the teaching and learning process.
- It's about the skills a student possesses and needs to be successful (Seidman, 2011).
- Don't make it harder than it really is.
- RIFD your students so you can track them throughout their college attendance and know where they are at all times (just kidding!).

Acknowledgments

I would like to thank Kurt Schoch, my trusted colleague and friend. He provided valuable feedback that made this book worthy of publication. A special thanks to Linda Serra Hagedorn for her insightful comments throughout. Her comments helped me shape ideas and make for a better presentation.

I would like to also thank those who have sat through my countless presentations of my formula and model and who have asked questions that helped me hone them. Additionally, I would like to thank the students who have used my formula, $Ret = Early_{ID} + (E + In + C)_{IV}$—that is, Retention = Early Identification + (Early + Intensive + Continuous) Intervention as the theoretical foundation for their dissertations. For the most part they have found positive results; that is very encouraging.

Those that did not I can only say that perhaps the intervention was not powerful enough to affect change since I know of no college that has fully implemented the formula and model. Finally, I thank you, the reader of this book, for giving me the opportunity to present my formula and model, which I hope you will adopt and help your students achieve their academic and personal goals.

Introduction

I am passionate about college student retention. Back in the stone age when I attended college, at the opening convocation in the gymnasium the dean would tell us to look to the right and to the left. He said one of us would not make it through to graduation. Since I graduated from high school Cuma Dentura, or by the skin of my teeth, as Dr. Joseph Hankin, president emeritus of Westchester Community College, would say, I figured I would be that one not to succeed. Upon reflection, that was almost a mean thing to tell first-time students, setting them up for failure instead of telling them you will succeed, and we will help you in any way we can.

College student retention continues to be a vexing issue for colleges and universities. Although colleges have spent enormous sums of money on programs and services to help students persist, retention figures have not changed significantly over time. Naturally, if money was not spent on specific programs and services the retention and graduation rates may have been lower.

Recent retention programs and services have been targeting specific groups of students, such as first-in-college students and specific minority groups. Regardless, the retention and graduation rates have not changed significantly over time. A perusal of ACT, NCES, and Clearinghouse data indicate this assertion.

This book is for practitioners, and as such will not present much in the way of retention and attrition data and references, although some major researchers will be named and their theories presented. There are some data tables from NCES and other groups for illustration purposes.

You all know how your college or university is doing retaining first-generation and minority students and its relationship to national, state, and peer retention figures. Besides, you would not be reading this book if your retention numbers met your college goals and federal and state officials were not breathing down your neck to increase the number of students who start at your institution and complete a degree in a timely fashion.

It can be a scary time for college and university presidents who are being pushed to do more with less while increasing student success rates, as perceived by those who hold the purse strings. Overlooked is that most colleges really want to increase their success rates with the students they accept. A concept that has been overlooked—the college mission and how well they carry out that mission.

Rarely in the retention literature is there reference to college mission, profile of students enrolled, and how well colleges do with the type of students they enroll. But as will be explained later, a mission statement is a key factor for considering how many students accomplish her/his academic and personal goals. Philosophy does not have to follow finance, as so many colleges currently use it as a measure of success.

It does not have to be that way. There are some very simple steps that a college or university can take to help students persist until academic and/or personal goal attainment. The terms *academic* and/or *personal goals* are used throughout this book. A student need not obtain a degree to accomplish them and thus should not be counted as attrition if they met them upon leaving a college.

But that is an issue that will need to be addressed at a later time with federal and state educational offices and the public at large. If a student does not earn a degree, that does not mean that he or she did not learn what he or she wanted to learn during the time of college enrollment. This should be noted in your retention figures; that is, the number of students who left prior to degree attainment but have gained the skills they wanted when they enrolled at your institution. This can make a difference in college and university retention figures and would be interesting to track. But I digress.

This book is intended to give the reader the necessary tools to implement a retention formula and success model that will actually help students meet their academic and personal goals and thus increase college retention and graduation rates. It is not as complicated as you might think and can be implemented using the resources you have on campus—faculty, administration, staff, and of course your number-one commodity, students. And it does not have to cost much money.

Following this path will help students accomplish their academic and/or personal goals and colleges to accomplish their stated missions. The challenge is to take the plunge of faith and marshal the campus community to become a part of the solution to the retention and graduation issue.

Remember, if you accept a student to your college or university, you have an obligation (moral/fiduciary), in my opinion, to provide programs and services to help the student obtain her/his academic and/or personal goals. This applies to all institutional types from the community college through the college and university, undergraduates to graduate students, professional schools, and more. Otherwise, why accept the student in the first place? Philosophy does not have to follow finance!

As a side bar: A college and university have the data available now to judge if a student who applies is accepted and enrolls but will have difficulty and need help. A college or university can develop a profile of the unsuccessful student who left for various reasons. When a student with a similar profile applies, is accepted and enrolls, it does not take much thought to make the leap that the student most likely would have difficulties at the institution. Intervention programs can be implemented for these students to help them succeed, but then again this does not deal with the systemic problem of helping all students meet their academic and personal goals at college entry. So, read on!

In addition, the Seidman student success formula and model that will be presented can be used for all types of educational institutions and delivery systems. It can be used for the traditional-age student (that will be the student I will be focusing on) at the brick-and-mortar college and university to nontraditional students, online colleges and universities, minorities, hybrid institutions (brick and mortar/online), graduate students, and more. You name the group and this system can be useful and work.

So, I encourage the reader to keep an open mind while reading; use your current knowledge of college student retention at your college. Think how you can implement what is discussed in this book. Do not assign a cost estimate to the process until you finish reading and have time to digest the material.

All too often we jump to conclusions and blow off ideas and suggestions by saying it will cost too much money to research and plan for. Remember that retaining a student over time will actually increase revenue. So, putting money upfront will come back many times over, and most importantly will help students accomplish their academic and/or personal goals and your college will fulfill its mission. The better the retention and graduation percentages are for a college, the more students will want to attend that college.

To provide context for the necessity to help students accomplish their academic and personal goals, a quick look at graduation rates sheds light on the problem. Each college can see where they fit into the numbers provided, but keep in mind this data is for students that started and finished at the same institution.

The U.S. Department of Education tracks graduation rates for students at four-year institutions for 150 percent of the time to graduate, or over a six-year period. They found 59.6 percent of full-time, first-time students at four-year institutions in 2008 who were seeking a bachelor's or equivalent degree completed a bachelor's or equivalent degree within six years (by 2014) at the institution where they began their studies.

For public institutions, the graduation rate was 58.5 percent, private institutions 65.4 percent, and at private, for-profit institutions 26.5 percent (Ginder, Kelly-Reid, and Mann, 2015). Additionally, when looking at the two-year college sector after attending 150 percent or three years, the graduation rate was 30.7 percent for all institutions; 21.8 for public institutions, 53.8 for private institutions, and 59.7 percent for private, for-profit institutions (Ginder, Kelly-Reid, and Mann, 2015).

These data are only to put the retention issue into context. Regardless of the academic ability, socioeconomic status, gender, first generation, and ethnicity of students, the Seidman retention formula and model that will be presented will help each and every college student type increase student retention and graduation rates. Most importantly, students will meet their academic and personal goals, colleges will be fulfilling their missions, and legislators, both national and state, will be happy and give more money to your institution. After all, by increasing student success it will enable our economy to grow, and successful students will beget other students to enroll at your institution—a win-win situation, something we all strive for.

So, keep an open mind, digest the material here within, and think about how you will organize your teams to implement the steps presented and how it will benefit your students. After all, isn't that what education is all about—giving people the tools to do what they want to do and a blueprint that she or he can use to obtain future education seamlessly? And always remember what Seidman says: "Don't make it harder than it really is!"

Chapter One

Why We Should Care about Retention

Why should we care about college student retention? After all, a student who leaves your college prior to completing a degree can be replaced with a transfer student. It has been told that it is less expensive to recruit a new student than to retain a student. This may be the case, but we are talking about human capital, and those we want to help contribute to our society both economically and socially. Retaining students until academic and/or goal attainment should be a priority of all colleges interested in serving the public good.

When a student applies to a college or university and is accepted, she or he should have a reasonable expectation that she or he will be provided with the programs and services to be successful. After all, the college or university should not have admitted the student unless there was a reasonable expectation that the student would be successful. Otherwise, why would the college or university accept the student in the first place?

All too often it may be for revenue purposes. After all, without sufficient funds the college would not exist or have to cut back on programs and services. Admissions offices are under a lot of pressure to make enrollment goals for first-year students to help balance the college budget. Unfortunately, philosophy follows finance perhaps instead of the other way around.

Years ago, there was a prediction of lower college enrollments due to a demographic shift in the high school graduating classes. In fact, this is happening again. The days of plenty of students are past. Less-selective colleges had to decide whether to loosen entry criteria to enroll the same or more students than in the past, keep entry criteria the same and expect the possibility of less students, or reduce the number of students without altering entry requirements. Those that lowered their entry requirements found that their retention and graduation rates plummeted while those that held the requirements steady

1

or lowered enrollment goals came through the dip in high school graduates just fine.

There is also the case of the college playing the selectivity game. It is assumed that a student would rather attend a selective college rather than a less selective one. So how can a college play the selectivity game to its advantage? Easy. Encourage student applications regardless of student suitability for acceptance both academically and socially.

The selectivity of a college, in most cases, is the number of applications versus acceptances; for instance, that one hundred applications and accept fifty of those applicants. That gives a selectivity index of 50 percent of those who apply and are accepted. So, the more applications the better the selectivity of a college, even if students are encouraged to apply even though they have no chance of acceptance.

Another way to judge a college is by yield rate. That is acceptance to enrolled. This is figured by the number of qualified accepted students, say one hundred, and the number who actually enroll, fifteen. That gives a yield of accepted to enrolled of 15 percent. This is not very high.

If a college needs an entering class of two thousand new students to balance the college budget, you can do the math in this scenario as to the number that needs to be accepted to meet that goal. Most colleges keep very good statistics as to the application to acceptance and acceptance to enrolled, or the yield rates as the admissions cycle progresses. Naturally, the lower acceptance rate and a higher yield rate the more selective the college and possibly more desirable to parents and students.

It is interesting that parents and students value the name of a college. In addition, parents and students like to apply to many colleges so they can tell others of the number of colleges their son or daughter was accepted into. What does not seem to be valued is the strength of the curriculum that a student wants to take.

Most parents and students do not ask for a college's study of the graduates to see if a student in a particular program gets jobs in the field upon graduation. Also, the study of the graduates usually contains starting salaries as well. So, it makes it possible to calculate the cost benefit of attending a particular college in a specific program: cost of college attendance and starting salary in a field.

It is reported in the Almanac issue of the *Chronicle of Higher Education* (2016) that students are applying to many colleges. That is, besides their first-choice college, students are applying to another one to five colleges at a 53.2 percent rate and six to ten additional colleges at a 28.7 percent rare. Regardless of the number of colleges applied to and accepted, 75.5 percent enrolled in their first-choice college. It is also interesting to note that for the most part students stay close to home, with 49.9 percent attending a college between one and one hundred miles from home with 29.4 percent attending a college one hundred and one to five hundred miles from home.

It would seem a better solution to tell students up front the profile of an accepted student and the percentage of those students who stay and graduate. That can easily be done. That is, tell interested students the profile of an accepted and graduated student.

This will help the student decide whether she or he meets the profile and to apply to that particular institution. Additionally, let students know the atmosphere of the college so they can determine if that is the atmosphere she or he wants in a college. The part that is not so easy, until you read the rest of this book, is providing programs and services for the student to be successful and meet her/his academic and personal goals and be comfortable with the college climate.

It should be noted that few colleges accept less than 50 percent of the students who apply. These are the highly sought-after colleges. These colleges perpetuate themselves by continually receiving an inordinate number of applications, so they can pick and choose who they deem the best and the brightest and add value to the college atmosphere.

There are many local colleges that provide superior education for students that are overlooked due to the desire of parents to have their son or daughter attend a highly selective college. This will not change anytime soon, so for those colleges that are less selective it is imperative that students are retained until they achieve academic and personal goals.

Colleges and universities keep a lot of data on the students who apply, are accepted, and enroll at their institutions. Therefore, colleges and universities should have the profiles of successful and unsuccessful students. It would then follow that colleges should only accept those that will be successful or at least have the chance of being successful. This also applies to the community college where the Ability to Benefit (ATB) from the educational experience can be used and is discussed in a later chapter.

If colleges accept and enroll those with a successful student profile, it then follows that the student should, theoretically, be successful. However, in some educational circles, unfortunately, "philosophy sometimes follows finance" instead of the other way around, "finance follows philosophy." College presidents lead colleges and are stewards of the programs of study and are charged with keeping the college economically viable. State system college presidents not only report to their Boards of Trustees but also to the state legislatures and must follow federal and state governmental regulations. Quite a balancing act. At least if there is a shortfall in funding they can go back to their state legislatures and beg for additional money.

This is not the case for the private educational sector. For the most part funding comes from tuition and federal financial aid money—grants and more. Some states do contribute to private educational institutions, but not so much as they do to their state institutions. So, if there is a shortfall in enrollments, revenue is diminished. Diminished revenue can lead to cutbacks of programs and services to students and increased class size can lead to neglect of infrastructure, causing a downward spiral that can be hard to reverse.

But more importantly is the college that follows its mission statement. Are colleges straying from their missions to ensure fiscal viability over student suitability? That is, what is the mission of the college, and is the college being true to its mission? It may very well be to enroll those that enter at whatever academic level and help the student gain the necessary academic skills to be successful. This, of course, is a noble endeavor, but still, if this is the case, then the college needs to provide the appropriate programs and services to help the student succeed.

Unfortunately, federal and state governmental agencies are judging colleges by their outcomes, those students who enroll and graduate within a specific time frame. Additionally, federal and state agencies look at the full-time, first-time student who enrolls in the fall term directly after graduating from high school. What is being lost is how colleges are doing relative to their mission.

This definition also does not consider the student who leaves after attaining her/his academic and personal goals without earning a degree. Nor does it consider a student who enrolls in the spring term and graduates in less than six years, nor the large number of students who are enrolled part time.

Not providing the appropriate programs and services to help a student succeed can be problematic to the student who will not gain the necessary skills to be successful and leave the institution prematurely, prior to academic and personal goal attainment. Since most of attrition occurs during the first term and year of college, student clock time is lost if the student is not successful.

LOSS OF TIME: THE NONRENEWABLE RESOURCE

Time is the great equalizer. Everyone, regardless of intellect or economic status, has 168 hours per week to do what she or he wants to do with it. And of course, time is a nonrenewable resource. When it is gone it cannot be renewed. Imagine spending fifteen weeks of a term or 2,520 hours and getting nothing out of it? That is quite a waste of time that may have been better spent elsewhere.

This happens to students who leave an institution without earning a degree or meeting their academic and/or personal goals. The longer a student stays and is unsuccessful the more time that cannot be reclaimed, not to mention financial aid and loans that must be repaid even if the student is not successful. Hence the student is left worse off than when she or he began college.

Not only has the student lost time but money as well. The debt burdens we place on our young adults will be carried forth by them over a long period of time. This can really hamper a person's ability to earn enough money to be a contributing member of our society.

UPGRADING OF SKILLS FOR JOB ADVANCEMENT OR SKILLS FOR ANOTHER JOB

Students who are turned off to the educational system may not take advantage of opportunities to upgrade their skills for job advancement. This then leads to an individual not progressing or "moving up the ladder" in their current place of employment. This can cause frustration and employee dissatisfaction. Additionally, if a person wants to apply for another job and does not seek out the skills necessary for that job, then the chances of getting the new job are greatly diminished. This can cause stagnation in the current employment situation and lead the employee to not perform at an optimum level; that is, a dissatisfied employee.

FUTURE EDUCATIONAL OPPORTUNITIES

Those that do not complete their education can therefore be turned off to future educational opportunities whether for job advancement, a new job application, or simply for enjoyment. The thirst for learning is within us all, but taking advantage of those learning opportunities can include taking a course or through a structured means through the internet. This then can stifle individual curiosity and wanting to gain new knowledge. It leads to the status quo.

A lack of education is a lack of training to decipher the myriad of information generated through the news media, internet, and other sources. Not being able to critically think and distinguish fact from fiction, manipulation from reality, hurts our ability at discourse on important matters that affect not only us but also our nation as a whole. Lack of education or even wanting to gain additional education leads to a citizenry that has knee-jerk reactions to current events and stifles critical thinking and questioning the wisdom of discourse.

Being able to listen to debate and then researching the facts can lead to a society that values the truth. Education gives us the ability to argue intelligently. Education gives us the ability to change our views. Education and the thirst for knowledge will lead us to breakthroughs that can better our society.

UNHAPPY STUDENTS TELL
OTHERS OF THEIR EXPERIENCE

Additionally, unhappy students tell others of their disillusioned experience at your college or university. Many colleges do not live up to the literature and admissions representative's views of the college. Many times, prospective students do not get a feel for the nature of the college; that is what the environment really is like.

Case in point. A college located in an area with few minorities in a very cold and snowy winter setting was instructed by the state education department that it needed to diversify its student body. In response, the college sent buses and recruiters to the southern part of the state where there was a large minority population.

This part of the state, although experienced in wintry weather and snow, was not nearly as cold and snowy as the college location. Students were bused to the campus and stayed overnight and were wined and dined and told how the college would provide a wonderful education. Which it could. The excursion took place in the early summer when the trees were in bloom and the area is quite beautiful.

Several minority students took advantage of the admissions offer and enrolled at the college. During the first few weeks these minority students went into town for various reasons. They found no one who looked like them; rather, people looked at them. The weather turned, and it was –20 degrees with three feet of snow.

Needless to say, the students did not return for a second term. They did not recommend this college to their friends. Not because of the education provided, but rather due to the nature of the weather and characteristics of the surrounding area.

Moral of the story? There are many well-meaning intentions. We all want a diverse student body. But you must be up front about the characteristics of your institution and town if you want to draw a diverse clientele. Providing extra support for these students may have helped them adjust to the college and its surroundings.

In college administration, you mostly hear about the bad stuff but rarely the good things that are done to help students succeed. As such, bad PR from students may impact the college's ability to recruit students to its campus. With social media, it is quite easy for a student to disparage a college or university for its lack of student support.

Nobody wants that kind of dialogue on social media to "go viral"! Trying to counter this type of publicity is hard since most will not believe the administration story, so it is best to let the issues drop or counter with satisfied students or the statistics that demonstrate that students you admit to your college graduate and find jobs in their selected programs. A good and comprehensive study of the graduates is a must.

When presenting at a conference, a person once said that it is more cost effective at his college to recruit another student than to save one. This, of course, was an astonishing statement since we are talking about human capital, not widgets. The misconception that it is cheaper to recruit another student than to save one is wrongheaded since the economic impact to the student without a college degree is significant than her/his peer with one.

Sure, on paper it may well be less expensive to recruit another student or take an extra transfer student than to provide programs and services to the student you accepted in the first place. But in the long run, spending money up front and graduating a student will generate more revenue. And need us not remember our college missions.

The statistics have shown for years that earning power decreases over a lifetime among those without a college degree. That is, a high school graduate will earn more money over a lifetime than a student without a high school diploma, and a college graduate will earn significantly more money over a lifetime than a high school graduate. In fact, upfront spending for proper stu-

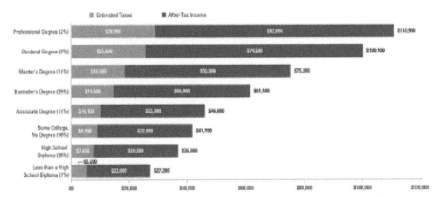

Figure 1.1.　Median Earnings and Tax Payments of Full-Time, Year-Round Workers Age 25 and Older, by Education Level, 2015.
The College Board, *Education Pays 2016*, Figure 2.1.

dent services will pay off to colleges in the long run. Do the math: If a student leaves after the first term, what is the cost in lost revenue over the next seven terms? Include auxiliary services and community spending.

The lost tuition and fees for a college are substantial. Although the loss of revenue can be great, it appears that many colleges are unwilling or not ready to put money up front to help students succeed. Colleges seem scared to commit the money necessary up front because if the interventions do not work, they have lost a substantial amount of money.

It behooves colleges to put their money where their acceptance is and provide the programs and services necessary for a student to be successful. See the box below of cost to colleges for student attrition. Remember that the majority of attrition happens after the first term and first year. You can plug in your own numbers.

Not only does a college lose tuition and fee revenue but auxiliary services money as well. This includes housing, the bookstore, food services, and more, who also lose revenue when a student leaves a college prematurely. The local community also loses revenue.

When a student leaves prematurely, the community will not reap hotel fees for family visits, room rentals for students living off campus, restaurants, recreational activities, and more. In addition, commuters will not need gas for their cars. So, the impact of losing students not only impacts the college but also the surrounding "college town" and state for those who leave that are from out of state. Remember, out-of-state tuition is usually much higher than that for in-state students.

Leaving college early dearly affects the student who borrowed money to help pay for her/his education. Regardless whether or not she or he got any-

---

LOST TUITION AND FEES, AN EXAMPLE

Cost of tuition and fees $5,000 per term (example).

If only 10 students leave after one term, the loss per term is:

- $ 50,000 per term or
- $350,000 for seven terms

If 50 students leave after one term, the loss per term is:

- $ 250,000 per term or
- $1,750,000 for seven terms

thing for the college experience, the loan must be repaid. If a student leaves the college due to a bad experience or mismatch with the college, the loan still has to be repaid.

Not receiving an education may make it harder to find a good-paying job, which in turn makes it more difficult to repay the loan. Not being able to repay the loan on time can affect future borrowing for a car or house. It can affect a person's credit rating and cause the individual to actually pay a higher rate for a secured loan. The student and perhaps parent who secured the loan in the first place are all losers in this scenario.

Figure 1.2 shows the average amount of financial aid awarded to first-time, full-time undergraduate students at four-year, degree-granting postsecondary institutions by type of financial aid and control of institution. The amounts borrowed are substantial, and if a student leaves the college after one term or year the loan has to be repaid with interest.

Figure 1.3 shows the accumulated amount borrowed by students at various institutional types over a four-year period. Even if a student graduates, the amount owed with interest is substantial. Many students seem to work to pay off their loans and delay marriage and buying a car or house. This, of course, affects our economy. The borrowing agencies benefit while the student and economy do not.

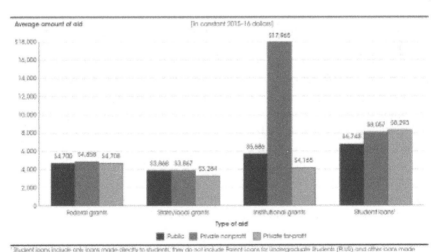

Figure 1.2. Financial Aid Awarded.
U.S. Department of Education, National Center for Educational Statistics, Integrated Postsecondary Educational Data System (IPEDS), Winter 2015–2016.

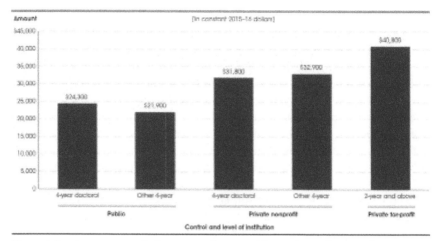

Figure 1.3. Average cumulative amount borrowed for undergraduate students.
Ginder, Kelly-Reid, and Mann (2015).

The cost of attending college keeps increasing, and the amount of student debt also has increased. The average first-year college tuition and grant and scholarship aid for students attending four-year public colleges was $19,022 and $6,928, respectively. For nonprofit private college, the costs are $37,260 and $15,858, respectively, and for-profit colleges $27,250 and $5,370, respectively (Ginder, Kelly-Reid, and Mann, 2015).

The cost of attending a public two-year college averages $12,104 and $4,700 in grant and scholarship aid. For private two-year colleges the costs are $24,595 and $5,747 and for-profit colleges $25,401 and $5,244 (Ginder, Kelly-Reid, and Mann, 2015). Now some will say that the figure just cited along with the tables do not match. True, as with all statistics they are open to interpretation, and it depends on the data set being used. Regardless, the cost of attendance and financial aid received is substantial and growing.

So, should we care about college student retention? Of course, we should. The consequences of not caring can affect the earning power of an individual. It can affect self-esteem as well. It can stifle productivity by not having an educated workforce or allowing an individual to take advantage of skill upgrades and job advancement. We as a nation should care about college student retention.

COST TO COLLEGES

Noted earlier is the monetary cost to colleges losing a student can be substantial, especially when you factor in the cost of recruiting a student to your college. Naturally, the recruitment cost can be recouped through tuition revenue, but losing a student after the first term can diminish your return on investment.

Case in point. If your tuition is $10,000 per term and you lose a student after the first year, you have gained $20,000 from that student but lost $60,000 for the three years of tuition revenue you would have gotten if the student stayed and graduated after four years. If this is the case for only ten students, the lost revenue is $600,000. This does not even count auxillary revenue from residence halls, food service, and spending in the surrounding community. You get the point.

So, spending money up front and adopting the Seidman retention formula and model will enable a college to gain much more revenue than was lost to students leaving prematurely. As you will note in the next chapter, keeping students through academic and personal goal completion will also enable a college to meet its mission. Remember that the mission of a college is why it exists. Do not write a fancy mission statement to satisfy accreditors or for public consumption; rather, write a mission statement that is meaningful and will enable a college to meet its public obligations.

Key ideas of chapter 1 are why we should care about college student retention. Topics covered include: loss of time, the nonrenewable resource; the need for upgrading of skills; wanting to take advantage of future educational opportunities; how unhappy students can affect college enrollments; and the cost to colleges of student attrition loss.

Chapter Two

The College Mission Statement

Not too many years ago, accrediting agencies first asked for college mission statements. Colleges formed task forces to develop them in response since they were now part of the accrediting process. It seemed, at the time to some, to be an exercise that did not seem important. It was thought that it was not necessary to pay attention to college mission statements since we who worked in a college know our student population and what we were trying to accomplish.

Mission statements just seemed to be something written simply to be available to accrediting agencies for accreditation purposes. Or it was for the public, state, and federal governments' consumption. Something to be available upon request but not really an important process of the educational system. But over time, the college mission statement has become very important.

Nowadays, colleges spend a lot of time crafting a mission statement. They can be meticulously crafted. Reviewing college mission statements can really give the essence of why a college exists, what they are all about, or what they are trying to accomplish with their students. The mission statement tells you who the college is targeting and how they will educate those they target.

Some colleges overdo the statement, trying to capture every single thing the college attempts to accomplish with different student types—directly out of high school students, returning students, minority, and nontraditional students. Some mission statements are paragraphs long, seemingly never-ending with goals and objectives listed that make them even longer and more complicated and difficult for the layperson to understand.

It seems if a college includes every one of its constituent groups in its mission statement so that they are covering all bases for their accrediting agency, local, state, and federal agencies. Then there are the one- or two-sentence mission statements that really capture the essence of the college's role in the education process and toward the betterment of society. These are easily understood and stand out in relationship to much longer mission statements.

It is an uncertainty whether students, faculty, staff, and administrators know their college mission statement or even care about it. If they do know the basic mission of the college, it is uncertain whether students, faculty, staff, and administrators take their mission statements seriously. On some college campuses, the college mission statement is prominently displayed in various places on campus. But if asked, students, faculty, staff, or administrators cannot recite the college mission statement or tell you what benefit the college provides for the public good.

Case in point. When giving a presentation, the speaker challenged the audience to recite their college mission statement word for word without looking it up. The giveaway was a $2 bill for the person who can recite their college mission statement word for word. In over fifteen years of doing this, only two $2 bills were given away.

The mission statement question has been asked in front of college presidents and numerous faculty members and staff, and not many can recite it, although most do know the essence of the mission statement meaning. Although that is a good thing, the college mission statement should set the tone for the educational experience a student will receive.

Not only should a college mission statement be prominently displayed, it should be discussed at faculty events and student orientation. The college community should be aware of the college's mission and be able to articulate it to anyone who asks. Faculty, students, administrators, and staff should live and breathe the colleges' mission statement.

A college mission statement is so important since it tells the world what a college stands for, why you exist, and the outcomes you wish your students to accomplish when they leave. Long mission statements are ones that no one is going to read, let alone understand. Having a short, succinct, to-the-point mission statement that you and the campus community can recite to others makes it understandable.

This is particularly important for prospective students. A prospective student should know why you exist and what you expect of and from them as they pursue their education. Hand out copies of the mission statement at orientation, and review and have discussions revolve around your commitment to students by reviewing the college mission statement. Never, ever be afraid to let everyone know who and what you represent as a college. Do not wait for reaccreditation to review and possibly revise your mission statement. Review your mission statement every three years and update or change as necessary. Then publish it for all to know. Be proud of what you want to accomplish as a college.

The key idea of chapter 2 was the importance of the college mission statement. It should not just be printed and displayed but given to students, faculty, staff, and administrators. Colloquia about the college mission statement should be held. College recruiters should make sure that potential applicants are versed in the mission of the college so they can make an educated choice whether the mission of a college meets their expectations.

Chapter Three

Student Institutional Fit

In our zeal to recruit students to our institution, we seem to overlook the concept of student institutional fit, which is derived from person-environmental fit theory. They are similar concepts. That is, if a student's environmental characteristics are dissimilar than those of the college, it may be difficult for the student to fit or assimilate socially, which can affect academics. But student institutional fit also can be associated with academics, to be discussed later.

College characteristics reflect the institution set by the administration, faculty, students, and location, both state and local. Let us first look at how this can affect the student institutional social fit. We know from Tinto's (1993) theoretical framework that not only is academic integration into the formal and informal systems of a college important, so is the social integration into the formal and informal systems as well.

The formal social systems of a college can include college-sponsored activities—weekly films, sponsored dances, lectures, sports activities both varsity and intramural, clubs and the like. Any extracurricular activity the college sets up is a formal social activity. The informal social activities can include groups forming sports events (basketball, baseball, ultimate frisbee), developing and supporting off-campus social events, fraternal organizations, and more student-to-student friendships.

We also know from the research that social integration is not as important as academic integration, but nonetheless it can influence student retention. This can be particularly problematic for a commuter and residential college. Commuter institutions are those that most students commute to each day to attend classes. Students can commute by car or in the city by bus or subway.

If a student is not told about the social atmosphere of the college, it can contribute to the student not becoming socially integrated into the formal and informal social systems of the college.

Case in point. A student may attend a college far from home, where going home on weekends is just not feasible on an ongoing basis. If the college is primarily a commuter institution, then the campus will empty out on the weekends, leaving little social activities for students in residence to partake in. A comparable situation can occur at a primarily residential campus. If a student is a commuter and attends a primarily residential campus, she or he may miss out on numerous weekend activities.

Another case in point. There are a lot of excellent institutions that have very restrictive social rules for a variety of reasons. Some do not allow smoking on campus in any place, have a dress code, dancing is not permitted, and neither is alcohol of any kind. If a student is unaware of these restrictions and she or he attends the institution, she or he may be in for a social shock if they expected otherwise.

Also alluded to earlier was the college in the far northern reaches of a state with no minorities at the college or in town being told they needed to diversify their campus. Recruiting students of color from the southern part of the state in the beautiful springtime enticed some to attend. With the first three-foot snowfall and minus temperature and no other similar color citizens in town, most of the students left the college.

This is not saying we want homogeneous campuses—diversity is a virtue—but there are ways to help minority students feel a part of the college and community. It takes a lot of effort to make this happen, but it is well worth the effort.

Academic integration into the formal and informal systems of a college are important for student retention. Formal system academic integration into a college means that a student attends classes, takes advantage of faculty office hours, and will seek out institutional help when necessary. The informal academic systems of a college can include meeting with faculty outside of the formal classroom, forming study groups with other students, and using campus services such as academic help centers, learning resource labs, computer centers, and other services.

Another important part of academic integration into the formal systems of a college is the academic profile or characteristics of enrolled students and where the student fits into that profile. For instance, see figure 3.1. It represents where a student theoretically falls on a college's enrolled student academic profile. The middle represents most students.

Theoretically those students whose academic profile falls within the norm or middle of enrolled students should find the work challenging but be able to earn sufficient grades to be successful. The student should also have some extra time to partake in academic and social activities.

A student at the high end of the academic spectrum for an enrolled student may find the coursework challenging but easier than the students in the

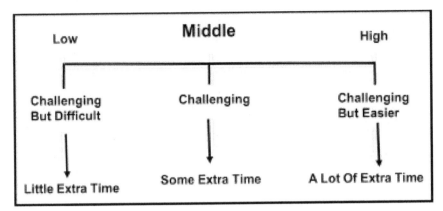

Figure 3.1.   Selectivity and Academic Activity.

middle, or majority of students. If the academic work is easy for the student, she or he will have a lot of extra time for academic and social activities. She or he may also have time for leadership positions within various academic and social activities. She or he will have more time to spend on something other than college activities.

The students at the low end of the spectrum of enrolled students may be students who applied to their "reach" school and were admitted. Perhaps the college did not have sufficient enough middle and high academic students to fill classes, so they reached down the academic ladder. A student in this category will find courses very challenging and difficult. This type of student will have little extra time to participate in academic and social enhancement activities.

Therefore, it is very important that students make an educated decision about which colleges are the best fit for them academically and socially. That is, students that attend the college have similar academic backgrounds and a good mix of social activities that match the interests of the applicant. Colleges need to provide this type of information—the academic profile of enrolled students and the social atmosphere of the college and college town—so students can make informed application decisions. This can only foster students applying to colleges that are the best academic and social fit.

The key idea of chapter 3 is the concept of college student academic and social "fit." That is, that the student and college have congruent academic and social identities. Students need to feel comfortable that enrolled students have similar academic backgrounds so they will be challenged academically but are not overwhelmed. Students need to feel comfortable socially knowing that they will fit and have similar values with the majority of other students who attend the college.

Chapter Four

Types of Student Departure

There are basically four types of student departure. Each one is very important and should be of concern to all colleges. They are: system, institutional, major, and course departure. System departure is from the educational system altogether. The student will never go back to college for a degree or certificate and therefore will not take courses to upgrade job skills or to learn new ones. Institutional departure is from a particular college and perhaps transferring or stopping out of college for a few terms but returning later to earn a degree. Major departure is from a particular major to another major or program. For example, a student transfers from a teaching program to a business program after going out into the field of teaching and not having a satisfactory experience. Or major change can be when a student has a career change of mind and switches majors. Course departure is when students depart from particular courses at a college. The course can be a course for majors or an elective course.

All are important, although colleges tend to focus on institutional departure. This is the student who is accepted to a college, enrolls, and leaves prior to academic and personal goal completion; that is, the student who leaves the college prematurely prior to earning a degree. Most student institutional departure occurs between the first and second term and the second and third term. That is early in the student's career at a college.

Why is this such a concern to colleges? Easy. There is a significant loss of revenue if a student leaves a college after the first or second term. See an earlier chapter on the money factor involved if a student leaves a college. Although this is the primary concern of a college, there are others that are also important and should not be overlooked.

Colleges should also be concerned with students who depart from a specific major and/or program. This could indicate a misplaced expectation of the major and its requirements and expectations. For instance, a student enrolls as an elementary education major, and after going to a practicum in an actual classroom setting changes her/his mind. Unfortunately, in this situation education practicum usually takes place in the third year.

If a student changes programs that late in their college career, it could mean additional time to review other career alternatives and time to complete a different career. That is why career development early on in a student's program is so important. Also shadowing a person in the proposed profession early on is important.

There are many issues associated with career choice and inappropriate career choice on the part of students and retention. To receive financial aid, a student must be in a degree program. Are we making students choose programs too early in their college career, so they meet this requirement? Do we assume that since a student chooses a specific major that is the career she or he will eventually end up with? Do colleges provide students with proactive career counseling to be sure that the program a student has chosen is the best fit with academic and personal abilities and skills?

Figure 4.1 from the Bureau of Labor Statistics shows the mean number of jobs held by individuals over a lifetime. It may be a surprise at how many jobs people hold over a lifetime and how important it is to provide students with career and job placement services.

The retention literature does tell us that undecided students leave college at a much greater rate than students with a defined career goal. It behooves a college to start the career exploration process early on and do not assume that a student knows what she or he wants to do simply because she or he chose a major. People change careers many times in their lifetime.

Colleges can do a lot to help students choose a career path, and they should. Helping students explore different career areas that can be related to initial choices can only help student career choice in the long run. Colleges can hold career exploration days where persons from different career areas can come to campus and talk to students regarding their career and how they made the

Characteristic	Total	0 or 1 job	2 to 4 jobs	5 to 7 jobs	8 to 10 jobs	11 to 14 jobs	15 or more jobs	Mean number of jobs held
Total	100.0	0.8	9.6	18.2	20.9	22.7	27.7	11.5
Less than a high school diploma	100.0	2.8	12.5	17.2	16.7	22.6	28.2	11.5
High school graduates, no college [1]	100.0	0.9	12.1	21.1	19.2	20.8	25.9	11.1
Some college or associate degree	100.0	0.3	8.0	17.1	20.5	21.6	32.5	12.3
Bachelor's degree and higher [2]	100.0	0.7	5.9	15.0	25.4	26.5	26.5	11.7

Figure 4.1. Number of Jobs Held by Individuals from Age Eighteen to Age Forty-Eight in 1978 to 2012 by Educational Attainment.
https://www.bls.gov/news.release/pdf/nlsoy.pdf.

choice to pursue it. This can be held in a large hall, gymnasium, or student center, where all career folks are together and students can shop around. This would be similar to college recruitment fairs.

Colleges can also have career exploration as part of orientation and/or ongoing orientation. Students can meet with similar students, faculty, and alums in their initial major during orientation. Additionally, career exploration can be built into the curriculum. Each course in a major can have a career exploration facet. There are different types of business administration careers, and they can be explored with each business-related course such as accounting, strategy, finance, and more. Majors can have guest speakers talk about their careers, why they chose the career path, and how they achieved their career goal.

Colleges can require students to visit and shadow a person in their intended major either prior to acceptance or as part of a first course in a major. Most job and career centers in colleges have career exploration software. This is an excellent way to have students also explore career choices.

Colleges also need to be concerned with a student leaving a particular course prematurely or are not prepared for the next-level course in a sequence. Once a student completes a foundation course, they usually take the next-level course in a sequence. Does the foundation course prepare the student for the next-level course in a sequence or program? Do courses in a sequence or program link to the next appropriate course? How do you determine if this is happening?

A case in point. Students were in a precollege math course that was to prepare them for the first college-level math course. Students who passed the precollege math course were then enrolled in the first college-level math course. Many students failed the first college-level math course. In theory, this should not happen if the precollege math course actually prepared a student for the first college math course.

The administration sought to determine the cause for these failures. It was discovered that most of the students who failed the first college-level math course were from the same precollege math course. The precollege math course instructor was contacted to try to ascertain why so many students from her/his section failed the first college-level math course. To the administration's astonishment, the precollege math course instructor indicated that she or he knew why so many of his precollege math course students were unprepared for the first level college course.

The instructor told the administration that they may recall that the weather was particularly severe during the term and that three class days were cancelled. Although there were make-up days, none included the missed math days. Therefore, the students were not able to complete the full course and missed concepts that would have given them the skills to be successful in the first college-level math course. Needless to say, the administration was stunned and changed its make-up day system so no courses would be missed any time in the future.

With the above in mind, colleges should monitor courses to see if certain course sections have higher rates of students not being able to successfully pass the next-level course. Perhaps students were misplaced in the course? Maybe the first course similar to the example above did not cover all that would prepare students for the next-level course. Perhaps the faculty member in the next-level course did not start the course where the students left off in the previous course. Colleges should make sure that courses link to one another so there is a smooth student transition to next-level courses.

Finally, and perhaps most importantly, is system departure; that is, from the educational system altogether. Tinto (1993) estimated that as many as 41 percent of students who drop out of college will never earn any type of degree; they are in essence dropping out of the educational system altogether. Even if the percentage is lower, this has profound consequences for the student and our society.

Mentioned earlier, this can cause a student to not upgrade his or her skills for current job advancement or to gain the necessary skills for another job. Many employers provide on-the-job training for employees. An employee who is turned off to the educational system may not participate or half-heartedly take advantage of work-related on-the-job training. Unhappy and undereducated workers may not put forth their best efforts on the job or gain income security.

There are two other factors that should concern colleges and universities when it comes to student departure. The two are voluntary and involuntary student departure. The one that usually concerns colleges the most is voluntary withdrawal; that is, when a student leaves on her/his own. These are the students who are dissatisfied with the current college experience and usually, but not always, become transfer students. Colleges need to discover why the student and college "fit" was inappropriate. It could have been a very simple reason, and if an early intervention was provided the student would have stayed at the college.

Tinto (1993) presented a theory of academic and social integration into the formal and informal aspects of a college. He posits that the more a student is integrated into the formal and informal academic and social systems of a college, the better chance that the student would persist.

A prime example of social integration (research tells us that academic integration is more important, but nonetheless) is the resident hall student who does not make her/his room her/his home. Their suitcase is not unpacked, there are no posters on the walls, the desk and computer not used, and more.

All it takes is for resident hall staff to visit each room the first few days of the term to ascertain which students do not seem to be adjusting to the college social environment.

Interventions can be developed to work with these students to help her/him adjust. Simple interventions such as discussing a student's concerns can make all the difference in the world to that student and help her/him overcome dissatisfaction with the college. Engagement of all students by faculty, administration, and staff can only help a student feel more at home at college. This does not seem to happen enough. Student, faculty, administration, and staff interaction should not occur randomly; it should be planned and executed carefully.

Involuntary departure is when a college dismisses a student for a variety of reasons. Most students will leave involuntarily due to academic issues, frequently because they are not meeting academic standard benchmarks. They can also be involuntarily dismissed for not complying with federal financial aid regulations of pursuit and progress. No money, no way to pay for education.

A student can also be involuntarily dismissed for social reasons, such as not adhering to the student code of conduct regulations. These students can be helped, especially those dismissed for academic issues. These students can be assigned peer tutors or even a summer session precourse at reduced rates. Remember, keeping a student for their full years to complete a degree will earn more money for the college than a student who leaves early. But most importantly, a college will be helping a student achieve her/his academic and personal goals and hopefully become a functioning member of society contributing to the social good.

Key ideas of chapter 4 were regarding different types of student departure from college. Discussed was system, institutional, major, and course departure. Also discussed was the distinction of voluntary and involuntary student college departure. The importance of career goals and selection was also discussed in this chapter, along with the importance of the student having a career goal in mind.

Chapter Five

Various Retention Risk Factors

There are many risk factors that have been identified in the literature that can have an adverse effect on student degree completion. These factors, which will be explained below, have not changed over time and should not be a surprise to those in the educational community. A review of those factors can help put into prospective what contributes as a roadblock to student college success. Colleges cannot do a lot to eliminate these risk factors, but awareness of them by faculty and staff can provide students with a sympathetic ear and perhaps some relief.

Delayed enrollment in college is an impediment to degree completion. That is, if a student does not enroll in college by the spring term after high school graduation, she or he has a higher likelihood of leaving college prematurely. Students in the lower income and academic levels may not believe that they have the finances to attend college. Those in lower academic achievement levels may not feel they are capable of being successful in college. These students, those in the lower economic and achievement level, may not have been encouraged to take challenging courses or guided toward college attendance.

The longer a person is out of school, learning begins to decay; that is, retention of academic material is lost. If a student is not motivated to continue to learn during nonschool time through reading and discourse with others, they may lose some of their earlier learning.

An exception to this is the student who takes a break to participate in some type of educational activity with all intentions of enrolling in college after the completion of the activity. This is known as the gap year, where usually well-to-do students participate or "find themselves" the summer prior to enrolling in college. These students have been accepted at a college and have deferred their enrollment.

Part-time attendance is also seen as a risk factor. A student may opt to attend college part time for a variety of reasons. A student may not want to commit to attending college full time, and she or he may want to "test the waters" to see what the college experience is about and if she or he can handle the academic rigor. Additionally, the student may have at home commitments such as taking care of aging parents and/or younger siblings.

Also, a part-time student may have to go to work to help pay home expenses or work odd hours. Since work will take priority over education, perhaps the student cannot devote the time necessary for studying. Maybe the working student is too tired to study, or perhaps the student has to work to pay for her/his education.

A financially independent student has a greater chance of noncompletion. This type of student is independent from parental or guardian control, and can be eighteen or older and out of the parent or guardian household. This student must pay for her/his own education. If this student receives financial aid, she or he may devote much of the money toward payment of rent or mortgage, food, clothing, and other expenses.

If the financially independent student has dependent children, this places another burden on the person. Not only may she or he share child-rearing responsibilities but also household chores and payment of food, clothing, and shelter. If the financially independent student is female, much of the care of the child and household chores may fall upon her. The care and welfare of children comes first in most parents' minds. If the choice is working on a paper due the next day or caring for a sick child, the choice is an obvious one.

Of note. We sometimes lack flexibility in our educational system since we try to treat all students equally even though they or their situations are not. This needs to change by valuing each individual student's needs and can be accomplished through student-faculty interaction or at the least intervention by staff in the know of a student's situation. This does not mean giving preferential treatment; it means taking into account the student's individual situation and being flexible on assignment due dates without penalty.

The burden of attendance of a single parent is greater than for that of a financially independent student, although they can be similar. However, a financially independent student may have another person in the household to help around the house and with the children. Being able to devote the time to studies when getting the children ready for school, dinner, homework, and more can place quite an obstacle in the way of student achievement in college.

If a child gets sick, it can place a single parent student in an unenviable situation; attending class or taking care of their child. Some single parents rely on others such as their parents to watch children. But it still does not take away the burden of not knowing what is transpiring in the house while the single parent is at school.

Additionally, providing for childcare for prior-to-school-age children or during regular school breaks can be a formidable obstacle. It can also be a financial burden, even though financial aid may be available. Indeed, many colleges have day care centers for student's children, but there is usually a cost associated with this care. In addition, many day care centers do not provide services for students above a certain age or the hours of operation do not coincide with college attendance. Some college day care centers close during college breaks, which does not do any good for the single parent who needs to also work.

A person without a high school diploma is less likely to persist than a person who is a high school graduate. This is due to the lack of skill acquisition before leaving high school. In addition, unfamiliarity with the rigors of reading and critically analyzing information can be lacking. Writing ability can also be stunted depending when the student left high school. It appears that the acquisition of a General Education Diploma (GED) does not cover the types of reading, writing, and critical-thinking skills that are necessary for student achievement in college.

Most, if not almost all, of these students require skill remediation. This prolongs entering college-level classes and can stigmatize the student in the eyes of her/his classmates. Not having a high school diploma will limit college choice for a student. Most four-year colleges will not admit this student and leave it to the community college for non–high school graduate skill acquisition.

Students are finding it difficult even with financial aid to attend college due to the cost. Many do not want to burden themselves with crushing debt that must be paid back over many years. They tend to get jobs and work part or full time. Working a forty-hour week and attending college full time does not leave time for much of anything else. A student working full-time shift work can have problems attending college.

The jobs many of these students take are low paying and are usually very demanding physically. Many are tired and find that they cannot keep up with both work and college. If it is feeding a family or themselves versus going to college, from Maslow's hierarchy of needs we know that food and shelter will win out over college attendance.

Of note. Many colleges have multiple sections of courses but are not flexible in letting a student move from one section to another during the term. Letting a student change course sections during a term due to unforeseen circumstances can solve many student issues. Counselors and faculty need to understand this and help facilitate course changes on their campuses.

Administration and faculty must also understand this phenomenon and be flexible enough to accommodate student needs. Most colleges say they are student centered, so this can demonstrate that claim.

Being the first in a family to attend college is a risk factor. Not having an example to follow to acculturate a student into the ethos of the college can cause early leaving. Also, being seen by peers as wanting to go to college can be a negative since others may be jealous of the student who wants to attend college. Peer pressure can be very daunting.

Not only does a first-generation student face many problems in attending a college, those from low socioeconomic areas attend college at a lower rate than their upper socioeconomic peers. This dovetails with familiarity with college attendance by older siblings and parents who instill in their children that they will attend college.

Most but not all students from first-generation and low socioeconomic areas are minority students. The schools they attend are usually in poor areas of a city, town, or state, and due to financial situations those schools often cannot afford to include advanced courses in the areas deemed essential to college student success such as English, writing, and mathematics. Therefore, even if a student is capable of high achievement, she or he may not be afforded the chance to take challenging courses since the school she or he attends cannot offer them.

Of note. A possible solution is presented later in this book to help alleviate this situation and help to even the playing field for first-generation and low socioeconomic students.

Key ideas of this chapter reviewed various student risk factors that keep a student from attending college or staying. The next chapter highlights what matters in college student retention.

Chapter Six

What Matters in College Student Retention

Numerous studies have identified what matters in college student retention. That is, what are the fundamental issues that predict student success or failure? The list has remained steady over the years, meaning that over the years what matters in college student retention has not changed over time.

Ever since college student retention has been studied, the number-one indicator of success has been and continues to be the rigor of the high school curriculum. This is the strongest indicator of degree completion. The more challenging courses a student takes in high school the greater the likelihood of college success.

This should not come as a surprise since the more academically ready a student is, the better prepared she or he is to handle the academic rigors of college work. This is consistent with the retention literature that student academic integration is more important than student social integration into a college. The academic preparedness of students has been touted by Astin (1993) and Seidman (2012) as the primary reason for student success. It takes precedence over social integration, although that is important also.

That is why the colleges that accept only the most highly academically prepared students also have the lowest attrition rate and the highest degree completion rates. Unfortunately, there are just so many high achievers to go around. Besides, colleges would not be meeting their missions if all they accepted and enrolled were the top students in the country or their state. This does not minimize the social integration aspect, but it just points out the importance of academic preparation as most significant.

Most colleges do not have the luxury of selecting the top academic students nationally, in their home state or locally. Most colleges accept more than 50 percent of those that apply to their college. An analogy can be drawn from the high school college sports world. Athletes are rated by their athletic ability in their sport of choice. Colleges then recruit those top athletes. Most of those top athletes will attend the college that will showcase their talents in hopeful preparation for a professional career.

It is well known that few of these top athletes who attend the top athletic colleges in their specialties will make the leap to the professional ranks. Nonetheless, these talented high school athletes will choose the college that will give her/him the best chance to showcase her/his talents. It is not that much different for academically talented high school students. These students will be recruited by the most selective of colleges and will attend the one that they feel will give them the best educational experience and the chance to showcase their academic abilities. This then gives them a huge advantage over the competition for the best jobs.

Of note. A student attends a top-ranked college and another attends a state college, both majoring in the business field. They both receive job offers from the same insurance company. The student who graduated from the top-ranked college receives salary X while the student who graduated from the state college receives a salary of –X.

After the first two years the student who graduated from the top-ranked college has sold $20,000,000 worth of insurance, while the student who graduated from the state college has sold $50,000,000. You can best bet which of these employees will advance quicker and earn more. *Moral of the story?* A degree from a top-ranked college may get you in the door at a good starting salary, but it is the production afterward that will determine future advancement and salary.

Even colleges that accept less than 50 percent of applicants does not guarantee degree completion. Even the most prestigious colleges have students who will leave prior to academic and personal goal completion. The fact remains that all colleges can have excellent retention and graduation rates.

Later on in this book you will learn how this can occur regardless of the types of students enrolled: high, medium, low achievers; rich, middle class, or poor; full time, part time; private, state, or for-profit college; from undergraduate to graduate programs.

Although academic preparation is the number-one factor in college success, there are others as well that also contribute to student success. And there can be a combination of two or more factors. For instance, a student who enrolls in college by the January after high school graduation increases their chances of degree completion than a student who enrolls in college later.

Some students take a term off to travel or work. Some may want to gain additional experiences or earn money. For many of these students, learning is still current, and motivation can still be high to attend and achieve in college. It is a fact that over time a person will forget some of what she or he has learned, but taking a term off does not seem to affect the learning process.

Earning at least twenty credits by the end of the first year (four-year college) is important for student success. Those students who earned less, only 22 percent earned a degree. Although earning at least ten credits per term, or less than the standard twelve credits for full-time attendance, does not seem like a lot, it is according to the research. This does not mean that a student did not take additional credits each term, it means that earning a least twenty credits by the end of the first year or two terms on a semester basis is important.

Therefore, it is important that colleges monitor average number of credits taken and earned per term, especially for full-time students. Colleges can intervene proactively with a student if she or he is not taking or earning enough credits during the first term to end up with twenty college credits earned after two terms. A student who will earn less than twenty credits the first year can be encouraged to take courses during the summer term.

It is incumbent to remember, if a student is not taking enough credits to earn a degree in four years, it prolongs the program and costs the student more money in the long run. Completing a degree taking the appropriate credits per term can help alleviate some of the financial burden for a student later on in life.

In relation to earning twenty credits after the first year, earning more than four credits during the summer correlated positively to degree completion. This is the case since a student can catch up if she or he did not take or earn enough credits during the regular terms. The student can also feel that she or he is making progress while taking courses during the summer months.

Most colleges offer several summer sessions, so the student does not have to take many courses in one summer session to catch up. Counseling intervention with the student can also help the student understand the importance of taking summer courses, which can translate into less terms to earn a degree, again saving the student money in the long term.

It is most interesting that switching majors did not influence degree completion but may delay graduation. It sounds counterintuitive, but the research demonstrates that it is not the case. This could be due to colleges having all students take a common core of courses during the first two years and selecting majors in the third year.

Counterintuitive thinking reminds of a *case in point*. A director of admissions at a community college accepted and enrolled over 250 students the first week of the term. All new students had to meet with a counselor to plan first-term courses. A counselor complained that the college was wasting valuable resources on these students who would fail out of the college after the first term due to their late enrollment and ability to catch up with work.

The director of admissions was put into a touchy situation since it is the job to enroll students, not bar them from attending. These 250-plus students represented many Full Time Equivalent (FTE) students, which translated into a considerable sum of state and local money for the college. The director of admissions's response to the counselor was to "prove it" that late accepted and enrolled students left at a greater rate than early enrollees. Although the counselor walked away very angry, it gave the director of admissions a sigh of relief since it would have been proven that these late enrollees would be the first to drop out and cause all sorts of enrollment issues for the college.

Lo and behold, the counselor decided to conduct a study to prove that these late enrollees did in fact drop out at a greater rate than the students who enrolled on time. The study results found that these late-enrolled students stayed at the college longer and had greater Grade Point Averages (GPA) than those students who registered prior to the first week of class. Why was this the case? The answer was quite simple. Read on.

Most, but not all, of these students were accepted and attended a four-year college and were very capable students. It turned out that once these students enrolled in their first-choice college they did not like the college atmosphere or living away from home. So, they left the original college during the first week, and not wanting to waste a term, they enrolled at their local community college.

The research also indicated that most of these students only stayed for one year and then transferred to another four-year college and were able to transfer all of their credits earned at the community college. They were indeed excellent students. This taught a valuable lesson: be sure to have data to back up claims, and let the data speak for itself.

Another case in point. A similar incident occurred on the Center for the Study of College Student Retention (www.cscs.org) website retention discussion group. With over one thousand members worldwide, one of the first questions received was about this very issue—allowing students to enroll the first week of classes. A member said that the faculty at her institution wanted to cut off admission prior to the first week since these students left the college at high rates. She also said there were no studies conducted about this issue.

Almost immediately three other discussion list members from three different institutions chimed in, saying they had a similar issue with faculty at their institutions. These discussion list members said that they conducted research on this very topic. They found, as was the case with the community college example, that these students were indeed the better students and would not stop enrolling them. With the data to back up their claims, the faculty who were skeptical were now most welcoming of these late enrollees. You never know where the data will lead and how contrary it may be to your initial thoughts.

The second year was deemed important for a student to catch up with the first-year lack of momentum. When a student could earn sufficient credit during the second year, she or he was able to catch up with her/his peers. This enabled the student to graduate in a timely fashion.

An interesting sidelight to the discussion in this chapter is that 60 percent of all students attended more than one college, and 35 percent attended more than two. This could include attending the community college, then transferring. It could include attending more than one community college or more than one four-year college.

This begs the question: How do colleges treat transfers? Do credits transfer easily from one college to another? Can a student enroll full time at a college and concurrently take a course at another college over the web or combination thereof? Can a student enroll at the home college for three courses, take a course at another local college, and a course over the web at a third college?

Have colleges taken these possibilities into account? Do they want to? Do they encourage or discourage the practice? Should colleges encourage or discourage students taking courses that are most convenient for themselves?

Today and in the future, students are not tied to one mode of learning. Should we be encouraging it? Should colleges do what is in the best interest of the student? How flexible should a college be to allow a student to tailor her/his own program with home college approval?

These are questions that need to be addressed and policies put in place. The more student centered and flexible a college is, the more benefits will occur for to their students. This does not mean accepting transfer credit if not warranted. It means working with other colleges to assist in easy transfer of credits. The point being that a student who is not satisfied with the initial college experience will, in some cases, leave the first college and attend another, more suitable college.

This, of course, is the concept of college student "fit" that was discussed earlier. That is, each college has its own culture, mores, and characteristics. Students with dissimilar characteristics as the college attending will not stay. This is not to say that a college should contain a set of homogeneous students, far from it. But it ports well that the student has something in kind or shared characteristics as the college attending. For example, a student who likes a social life that includes parties and other activities will not be attending a college for long that doesn't allow dancing or parties.

It is, therefore, important for a potential student to visit colleges to gauge the types of students who are in attendance and get a feel for the college atmosphere. Simply listening to college recruiters will not give the student a clear picture of life at the college. Prospective students should seek out students away from the formal tour. Ask questions, such as, What do you enjoy best about this college, and what do you like least? There are many other questions to ask that others have written about; thus it will not be covered here.

With all this said, the strongest indicator of degree completion is the rigor of the high school curriculum. Many parents insist that their child apply to their so-called reach college. That is, the student does not quite meet the qualifications of the mean that are admitted and attend the institution. Accepted and enrolled students will have specific academic qualities. They are on a continuum, whereas those students at the top of the academic qualifications will find the work challenging but doable with extra time for a variety of activities.

Those students at the mean will work harder and have less time for activities, while those students who barely meet the academic requirements will find it necessary to spend a lot of time in studies and little else. So, it would seem it is best to be at the mean of those enrolled in a college than at the low end.

Let us briefly look back at the fact that 60 percent of students attended more than one college and 35 percent attended more than two. This begs the question: How do you treat transfers or internal students that take mixed or blended courses? Many colleges distinguish between day and evening classes with a differential tuition, on campus versus off campus or on campus versus online offered by your college, or on your college campus versus online at another college.

Students have so many options, such as taking a course on campus at your institution, off campus at another institution, online course at your campus, or online course at another institution. This can include a combination such as on campus, day/evening, off campus, online at your campus or another college. Do you know how many, if any, of your students are doing this or if they want to have a variety of choices? How does this affect the student? Do you allow students to do this? If not, why not? Does it really matter if the student takes an approved course elsewhere or online? Do you encourage or discourage this type of education? It would behoove colleges to examine this phenomenon and develop student-friendly policies.

A key takeaway from this chapter is what matters in college student retention. The areas that were covered have not changed over time. As usual, the rigor of the courses taken in high school remains the number-one indicator of college success. The next chapter will delve into what we know about first-generation college students. This is a growing segment of the college population.

Chapter Seven

What We Know about First-Generation College Students

A first-generation college student is a student who is the first in her/his family to attend college. If the student is from a nuclear family, neither parent has attended college. If from a single parent/guardian family, the parent or guardian has not attended college.

Thus, a first-generation college student does not have an example to follow or been given guidance about what to expect from the college experience from her/his family. This would pertain to whether the student attends a local commuter college or lives away from home for the first time. They do not have a previous parent/guardian or sibling who can relate the difference in the academic rigor of college versus high school or various aspects such as personal independence, keeping a budget, and time management. Perhaps not having a high school guidance counselor hunting them down to make sure they are attending class and turning in homework might be most important.

Since first-generation college students make up a large portion of college enrollments and have high attrition rates, they have garnered attention by colleges to receive additional programs and services to help them succeed. Table 7.1 shows the percentage of first-year students who identified as first-generation in the annual Cooperative Institutional Research Program (CIRP) (2017) study. The annual CIRP study is the longest continuous annual assessment of first-year college students. It provides a good snapshot of student trends over time. According to the CIRP study:

> The proportion of students identifying as first-generation varies considerably by sex and race/ethnicity. . . . about one in five women (20.3%) identify as first-generation, slightly more than men (17.0%). Across race/ethnicity, nearly

Table 7.1.　Percent of Group Identifying as First-Generation

Women	20.3
Men	17.0
Native American	21.5
Asian American/Pacific Islander	18.2
Black	27.0
Latino	57.3
White	10.5
Other	29.1
Multiracial	17.3

three of five Latino students (57.3%) are first-generation, roughly double the proportions of students who identify their race as "other" (29.1%) and Black students (27.0%). By contrast, just 1 in 10 White students (10.5%) are first-generation. (11)

Additionally, according to the CIRP data, first-generation college students considered close proximity of college to home (within fifty miles) as a very important reason for choosing the college attended.

Most are familiar with Tinto's (1993) academic and social integration into the formal and informal aspects of a college as being important for student retention. But for many minorities, especially Latinos, family and being close to family is most important. Therefore, Latinos want to live near home and return to home after classes, so these students do not participate in the formal and informal social systems of the college, and this may lead to greater attrition among this group.

The CIRP (2017) study also indicated that many first-generation students intend to work twenty-plus hours per week to help pay for their education. Working part time can affect student academic performance with varying shifts and being tired from work and not being able to put forth a full effort on studying and coursework. Thus, first-generation students opt to attend a private college for reasons of size and financial assistance instead of state colleges.

Bridge programs usually offered the summer prior to enrollment have been developed to help a variety of students, including helping first-generation students adjust to college life. These programs usually have an academic component in reading, writing, and mathematics. The purpose of these academic classes is to try to make these students college ready in those important skill areas. There are also social integrative events that provide help for these students to engage in campus life. More regarding bridge programs will be discussed in a later chapter.

Key ideas of the chapter were the current percentage of first-generation students attending college. Latino/a college attendance has grown the fastest over the years. Also outlined were the causes of first-generation student departure and what can help first-generation students succeed. But presented later, a simple system can help all students succeed, and with little additional effort on the part of the college. The following chapter will discuss what we know about minority student retention.

Chapter Eight

What We Know about Minority Student Retention

Minority student college enrollment continues to increase as well as attrition figures for this group of students. Similar to first-generation students, colleges are taking a more active part in providing targeted programs and services to help minority students to succeed. Figure 8.1 shows the enrollment of minority students over time, from 2000 to 2015.

L. Musu-Gillette, J. Robinson, J. McFarland, A. KewalRamani, A. Zhang, and S. Wilkinson-Flicker, authors of the NCES *Status and Trends in the Education of Racial and Ethnic Groups 2016*, point out:

Of the 17.0 million undergraduate students in fall 2015, some 9.3 million were White, 3.0 million were Hispanic, 2.3 million were Black, 1.1 million were Asian/Pacific Islander, and 132,000 were American Indian/Alaska Native. Between 2000 and 2015, Hispanic enrollment more than doubled (a 126 percent increase from 1.4 million to 3.0 million students).

In contrast, enrollment for other racial/ethnic groups fluctuated during this period. Between 2000 and 2010, Black enrollment increased by 73 percent (from 1.5 million to 2.7 million students), Asian/Pacific Islander enrollment increased by 29 percent (from 846,000 to 1.1 million students), American Indian/Alaska Native enrollment increased by 29 percent (from 139,000 to 179,000 students), and White enrollment increased by 21 percent (from 9.0 million to 10.9 million students).

However, between 2010 and 2015, American Indian/Alaska Native enrollment decreased by 26 percent (from 179,000 to 132,000 students), White enrollment decreased by 15 percent (from 10.9 million to 9.3 million students), Black enrollment decreased by 14 percent (from 2.7 million to 2.3 million students), and Asian/Pacific Islander enrollment remained relatively unchanged (at 1.1 million students).

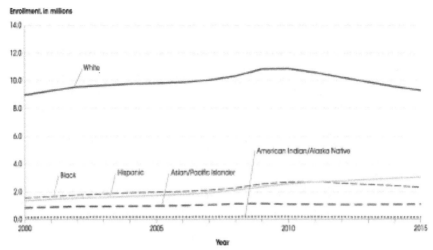

Figure 8.1. Undergraduate Enrollment in Degree-Granting Postsecondary Institutions, by Race/Ethnicity, Fall 2000–2015.
U.S. Department of Education, National Center for Education Statistics, Integrated Postsecondary Education Data System (IPEDS), Spring 2001 through Spring 2016, Fall Enrollment component. See Digest of Education Statistics 2005, table 205; Digest of Education Statistics 2009, table 226; Digest of Education Statistics 2015 and 2016, table 306.10.

Graduation rates for minorities have varied over time as well. From the data from NCES (2016) figure 8.2 below shows the following graduation information. Please note that the measure is for four-year colleges only and represents 150 percent of the time to graduate, or six years. Thus, the entering cohort of 2006 measures graduates of this cohort in 2012 and so forth.

The data in figure 8.2 is clear that minority students over time, except for Asian students, graduate at a lower rate than White students. Looking at the entering classes of 2006, 2007, and 2008, six years later there has not been much positive movement in graduation rates for minorities. This is in spite of additional programs and services implemented by colleges to help minority students succeed.

There have been many reasons identified for the minority retention rates to be lower than for White students. These include: lack of academic preparation, lack of a critical mass of students with similar ethnic characteristics on campus, initial enthusiasm displayed by recruitment process but subsequent disappointment once enrolled, and financial need.

Looking at each of these reasons gives a picture of the issues facing minority students graduating from college. Many minority students are in the lower economic status. Thus, the schools they attend lack supplies and textbooks and may not offer advanced courses in English and mathematics.

Time to completion, sex, control of institution, cohort entry year, and acceptance rate	Total	White	Black	Hispanic	Asian/Pacific Islander: Total	Asian	Pacific Islander	American Indian/Alaska Native	Two or more races	Non-resident alien
Graduating within 6 years after start, males and females										
All 4-year institutions										
2006 starting cohort	59.2	63.5	40.2	51.9	70.1	71.6	49.5	40.2	60.6	60.4
2007 starting cohort	59.4	62.8	40.1	52.3	70.6	70.5	49.3	40.6	61.8	61.9
2008 starting cohort	59.8	63.7	40.9	53.9	70.4	71.2	50.8	41.9	60.7	60.9
Public institutions										
2006 starting cohort	57.2	60.3	38.7	49.5	69.2	68.5	49.1	38.2	57.0	57.7
2007 starting cohort	57.1	60.7	40.3	50.7	68.9	68.3	49.8	38.5	60.0	58.3
2008 starting cohort	58.3	61.4	41.3	51.8	69.9	69.4	49.5	38.9	58.9	61.8
Nonprofit institutions										
2006 starting cohort	65.5	69.1	44.5	62.2	76.9	77.5	52.6	51.3	71.5	71.5
2007 starting cohort	65.3	69.3	44.5	60.9	77.6	77.5	57.6	47.8	56.8	76.5
2008 starting cohort	65.4	69.2	44.6	61.3	76.1	77.3	60.8	48.7	73.2	72.1
For-profit institutions										
2006 starting cohort	34.9	45.3	22.3	35.7	42.3	44.4	25.2	18.8	32.4	38.2
2007 starting cohort	31.9	40.0	23.4	35.8	41.3	47.8	31.9	14.6	32.5	41.1
2008 starting cohort	26.5	34.4	18.8	31.7	41.3	44.5	26.1	19.8	30.3	31.3

Figure 8.2. Graduation Rate from First Institution Attended for First-Time, Full-Time Bachelor's Degree-Seeking Students at Four-Year Postsecondary Institutions, by Race/Ethnicity, Time to Completion, and Control of Institution. Selected Cohort Entry Years, 2006 through 2009.

U.S. Department of Education, National Center for Education Statistics, Integrated Postsecondary Education Data System (IPEDS), Spring 2002 through Spring 2013 and Winter 2013–2014 through Winter 2015–2016, Graduation Rates component; and IPEDS Fall 2009, Institutional Characteristics component.

Although colleges are recruiting more minority students, there may not be enough to really form support groups or minority faculty as mentors. It is the job of admissions officers to recruit students to their colleges and try to enroll as diverse a student body as possible. This may lead to painting an unrealistic picture of the campus community and characteristics. A minority student may find what they were told by the admissions recruiter was not reality once reaching campus.

Additionally, since many minority students are from lower socioeconomic status, financial need becomes an issue. The financial aid system is usually very complicated, and dependent students need information from parents' income tax forms. Parents may not be able to supply this information on a timely basis; thus, these students may miss out on receiving the maximum financial aid. Also, if financial aid offices are not attuned to these students' needs and treat them similarly as majority students, it may turn them away from seeking help in filing financial aid forms.

We also know what can help minority students persist at colleges. These include: mentor programs, financial aid, groups and clubs for various minority groups, summer precollege academic programs, multicultural centers, and inclusive and meaningful curriculum.

Having a mentor with a similar background and is a successful student (college faculty member, fourth-year student) can help acculturate a student into the formal and informal academic and social systems of a college. Specific groups and clubs for minority students can give minority students that critical mass of similar students since they are usually not the majority ethnic group on campus.

Summer bridge programs can help minority students hone their academic skills in English, writing, and mathematics to prepare them for the rigors of the college curriculum. Multicultural centers where students of all ethnicities can meet and learn about each other's cultures can be an effective way to get students to learn about each other. An inclusive curriculum does not marginalize one ethnic group from another. Having a realistic curriculum that highlights the accomplishments of all ethnic groups can only help to bring all students together.

Also providing financial aid to alleviate the reliance of working too many hours to earn tuition and spending money can make a significant retention contribution to minority students. This aid in addition to federal and state money can come directly from the college as well. Giving minority students on-campus employment, or work study, can help inculcate the college culture. Various curriculum faculty working on various projects, articles, and more can have a student as an aid.

This contributes to mentoring and having the student participate in campus life. But most importantly it is providing the student money where she or he does not have to work off campus to earn money in an unrelated field. College foundations can and should raise money for this.

Key ideas of this chapter were the current percentage of minority students attending college. Latino/a college attendance has grown the fastest over the years. In addition, the graduation rates of students over time was also reviewed. Also outlined were the causes of minority student departure and what can help minority students succeed. But as will be outlined later, a simple system can help all students succeed and with little additional effort on the part of the college. The next chapter delves into other student considerations.

Chapter Nine

Other Considerations

When discussing college student retention, there are some other considerations a college needs to think about. One is defining retention that matches
your college mission. Another consideration is: Do you have a retention
problem? Also, is there such a thing as "good attrition"?

These will be covered briefly but are important considerations when thinking about college student retention. The goal, of course, is zero attrition. But
then again, that is not realistic. Maximizing retention and graduation of your
students is the key; providing programs and services that will help students
succeed is fundamental.

DEFINING RETENTION

So, what's in a definition? To get a handle on the retention and attrition rates,
a college first needs to define retention and attrition. We know that the federal
government requires colleges and universities to report certain information.
Specifically, the U.S. Department of Education (USDOE) asks colleges to
track the fall entering class of full-time, first-time students in a degree program over time and provide graduation data for students up to 150 percent of
the time to complete a degree.

This equates to six years for a four-year college and three years for a two-
year college to determine whether the student has completed the program and
earned a degree. Even though it is a flawed definition (it does not consider
part-time students or full-time students who start in a later term), it is the
definition colleges and universities must comply with or risk losing the ability
to receive and dispense federal financial aid.

The federal definition is flawed in several ways, especially when it only includes the full-time, first-time students who begin their education during a fall term. Students who are part time, which is a majority of community college students, are not counted. Students who begin their education in the second term are also not counted even if the student completes and earns a degree in four years' time or less. It is counterproductive, however, to question the merits of the federal definition. This definition has been hotly debated and will continue to be debated.

Additionally, many states' legislatures are either using the USDOE's definition of retention or their own when judging college success rates. The success rates once again are usually tied to graduation of students regardless of whether or not the student met her/his academic and social goals and left the college early.

Most of the time colleges and universities have no input into state definitions, and lawmakers do not really understand the nuances of student enrollments such as stop-outs—those who leave for a term or two and then return in good standing or begin a program other than the fall term. Sometimes these state definitions seem as arbitrary as the federal definition. Most often state definitions again try to have one size fit all without considering student ability at entry, the need for remediation, and full time versus part time and work requirements of students to obtain the funds necessary to attend college. Nor do they take into account the mission of the college.

Some states are eliminating remedial educational programs at colleges, although students may lack the requisite skills to be successful in courses with these programs. It is a money saver for publicly funded colleges, but does this cause colleges to water down introductory courses to accommodate unprepared students? Does it force students to attend a community college to build up their skills (which is not a bad thing)? How about the disillusion of remedial courses at the community college? Where does a student turn to develop critical skills necessary for success?

If students are forced to attend the community college to attain skills necessary to be successful at a four-year college, does this mean that community college enrollments will grow substantially and four-year college enrollments will plummet for at least the first two years? Does this then turn many four-year colleges into upper-division institutions? Also, what affect does this have on K–12 education? These are some of the basic questions that should be asked and addressed before a state or college eliminates remedial education programs.

So, are these the only definitions (federal and state) that a college can use to define college student retention? In addition to federal and state demands for retention data, can a college also define retention and attrition using its own definitions? Sure, why not?

Does your college have a separate definition than what is required by the federal and state governmental agencies? If you do not have your own retention definition, why not? Will it create extra work to gather the information, perhaps? Will it accurately reflect your college or university mission, perhaps? Once listed, can it become the definition that your state uses to judge your retention rates, perhaps?

Once it is listed and data driven, it may become, over time, the figure that is used to judge how the institution is doing regarding the retention of students it admits. But most importantly it will give an accurate picture of how the college or university is doing in its efforts to retain all students within the context of its mission. Your retention definition should be tied into the college mission; after all, that is why you exist as an educational institution.

A side note. It has always been interesting how many college administrators, faculty, staff, and students have no idea what is the mission of the college or university they work in or attended. At presentations at colleges, the question asked is, Who can recite the college mission statement word for word without looking it up? The reward is a $2 bill to whomever can do this. In about fifteen years of asking this question, only two $2 bills were given to those who knew their college mission statement word for word. The audiences challenged have had faculty, staff, and college presidents in attendance.

How many reading this can recite your college or university mission statement word for word without looking at it? Does the senior staff, faculty, students, and parents know it? Do not just have it pinned up on walls in offices and around campus; nobody looks at them.

Colleges should talk about its mission statement on campus as all administrators, faculty, staff, students, and parents should know what the college or university is trying to accomplish. Be proud of what you are trying to accomplish with your students. That is a good first step.

DO YOU HAVE A RETENTION PROBLEM?

Using your own retention and attrition definition, with justification for its use and tied in with your mission statement, what is your retention rate with the student population you serve? You can use data such as: first-to-second-term retention, term-to-term retention through graduation or leaving, and credits attempted and earned term to term (this will help you see how long it will take your students to earn a degree). Then you need to determine whether or not the student met her/his academic and personal goals when she or he left the institution either through graduation or on their own volition. You can then determine whether you have a retention issue based on your data and analysis in comparison with your mission statement.

Another important aspect of using your own retention definition is, What are your peers' (you should know them but be sure that they use the same retention definition you do) retention rates assuming similar missions? How do you compare? Why not get together with your peers and share retention definitions and agree on a common one that you all use to judge retention effectiveness?

Even if you are doing better than your peers, do you want to improve even more? You should. Your retention goal would be to have every (well most) student when she or he leaves be able to say that she or he accomplished what she or he came to accomplish when she or he entered your institution. And that may not be to earn a degree. Is this a fair statement?

If a student leaves your college prematurely, why? Is it something as simple as a $100 loan that would have kept the student enrolled? Was it difficulty with one class? Was it a personality issue with a faculty member, staff, or another student? Was it a social issue? Finding answers to these questions could help a student persist until academic and/or personal goal attainment. Using an exit interview, survey, or contacting the student by email or phone could help find the answers to these questions.

GOOD ATTRITION

Is there such a thing as good attrition? Well yes, of course there is. If a student enrolls in your college or university to obtain a specific goal(s) and left after accomplishing her/his goal(s) regardless if it is after one or more terms, then that student should not be considered a failure but rather a success and not considered attrition. If a student transfers to another institution because your college cannot meet her/his needs, is that a failure? Perhaps the student upon career exploration changes career goals and your college does not have the proper program of study and therefore transfers to a more appropriate college. Is that considered attrition, no? Again, it is important to gather the reason(s) why a student enrolls in your college or university in the first place. It is just as important to find out whether the student achieved their academic and personal goal(s) when she or he leaves your college.

This also works the other way around too. Simply since a student graduates from your college or university does not mean that the student achieved her/his academic and personal goal(s). Can this happen, why not? How many students graduate in one major and are employed in a totally different field? A perusal of your study of the graduates can help you determine this.

Again, degree interest at entry needs to be gathered and compared with exit data—the graduation degree. This will also show whether the student changed goal(s) between entry and leaving and if the goal(s) at leaving were met. This may also explain the length of time to meet degree requirements.

Additionally, what may affect retention is the number of times a student changes majors. It should not be a great surprise to a college that many students will change their majors once enrolled. It should behoove colleges to provide major specific programs for a student so she or he can really find out what is required in particular professions.

Case in point. In the education field, a student takes a semester practicum usually in their third year. Once in the practicum classroom the student may determine that she or he does not want to be a teacher. If the practicum occurred in the first year, then the student would not have lost time learning a field that she or he does not want to attain a degree in. Choosing another major may entail several additional terms, whereas if the practicum took place in the first term it may have minimized taking extra terms in another major.

It is therefore important to provide students with career information and perhaps shadow those in a chosen career as early as possible. This can then help a student decide whether the major or career of first choice is really what they intend to do upon graduation or goal completion. Many colleges have job and career centers. These are wonderful places that a student can gain useful information on her/his initial career choice. Also, there are many computer programs a student can take to see where their aptitude lies. Avenues should be established that encourage or require a student to explore her/his career choices.

So, as you can tell, the way that a college or university defines retention/ attrition is the key to whether you are doing well or want or need to do better. The way programs are structured can also affect retention by providing necessary information for a student to make an educated choice of major and career direction. Data should be collected at all stages of a student's educational career and programs and services provided to help the student select a major that is best suited for their aptitude and disposition. Never assume that a student really knows what their career will be upon graduation and years thereafter.

Key ideas of this chapter reviewed other retention considerations. The following chapter will review the most representative student enrollment model and why it does not work.

Chapter Ten

Most Representative Student Enrollment Model

Why It Does Not Work

There is a most representative student enrollment model that is used by most colleges. It is quite simple and has two branches. One is acceptance and assessment of reading, writing, and mathematical skills prior to enrollment. Based on the assessment results, students are placed either in college-level foundation courses or placed in non-college-level courses in the areas in need of remediation. The other is acceptance with no assessment and enrollment directly into college-level courses.

There can be a combination of college-level course placement as well as placement in a non-college-level remedial course. For example, a student has passed the reading and writing assessment at a level deemed college ready by the college, while mathematics assessment merits the need for remediation. So, the student can be placed in college-level foundation courses that require college-level reading and writing and a remedial course in mathematics.

The other representative student enrollment model is acceptance to the college and no assessment of student skills at entry. The student is placed into college-level foundation courses regardless of student skill levels in reading, writing, or mathematics. Many colleges who use this model may indicate that they only accept students who are college-course-level ready.

Unfortunately, the retention data does not bear out this assumption that the student is college ready without assessment. Only the 10 percent of colleges who accept and enroll the top students have very good retention and graduation rates. But if you have two enrollment models that have similar results—students leaving prior to academic and personal goal completion—what does this tell about your assessment and foundation courses? This will be covered a bit later in this discussion. Figure 10.1 illustrates the current student enrollment models.

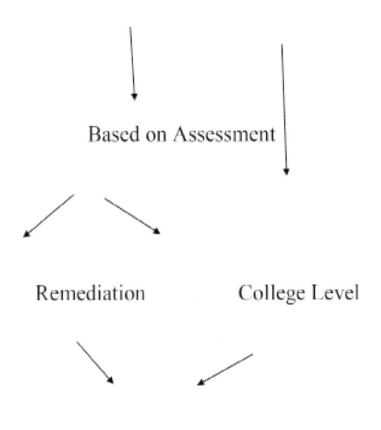

Figure 10.1. Current Student Enrollment Models.
Seidman et al. (2017).

There are several reasons why the most representative model of admissions and enrollment does not work. The most important one is that college assessment may or may not be assessing the skills necessary for a student to be successful in a foundation course. Additionally, remediation may or may not be remediating the skills that a student needs to be successful.

Simply assessing and assuming the assessment covers what is needed to be successful in a foundation course does not mean you are assessing the correct skills. Also, simply remediating and assuming the remediation covers what is needed to be successful in a course does not mean you are remediating the correct skills.

Colleges are assessing skills without knowing what skills to assess. *They are carrying out the process backward by assessing unknown skills and hoping that they match or meet the actual skills necessary to be successful in foundation courses.* In upcoming chapters, you will learn what needs to be done in easy, doable steps to ensure that students are assessed for needed skills to be successful in foundation courses and are delivered the skills necessary to be successful in those courses. This will enable students to meet their academic and personal goals.

Key ideas of this chapter reviewed the current enrollment placement of students at college entry and why it does not work. The next chapter will present the Seidman Student Success Formula/Model and five steps to student success.

Chapter Eleven

Seidman Student Success Formula/ Model and Five Steps to Success

Seidman says, "Don't make it any harder than it needs to be."

Colleges do not have to spend a lot of money to begin, continue, or to move to the next level retaining the students they recruited and enrolled. All colleges want to maximize their retention efforts. Shaprio et al. (2017) showed that:

> Nationally, 54.8 percent of students who started in any type of college or university in Fall 2010 completed a degree or certificate within six years. When examined by race and ethnicity, Asian and white students had a much higher completion rate (63.2 percent and 62.0 percent, respectively) than Hispanic and black students (45.8 percent and 38.0 percent, respectively). These rates include students who graduated after a transfer. (2)

U.S. retention figures have not improved much over time, even with substantial amounts of money expended on programs and services. Students are no better integrated into the formal and informal academic and social systems of colleges today than twenty years ago.

ACT has keep retention and graduation figures since 1982. Their graduation rates measure completion at five years since ACT (2017) started keeping this data prior to the federal government's definition of six years to graduate. ACT data indicates that for all types of four-year colleges (private and public) in 2004, 52.0 percent graduated after five years. In 2015 the graduation rate after five years was 52.6 percent. These figures are generally within 1 percent going back many years. Naturally, if you add a sixth-year graduation definition the rate increases but receives similar results.

It also needs to be noted that the more highly selective a college is the greater the graduation rate after five or six years. Not many colleges have the luxury of admitting only the very best high school graduates every year. In spite of this, even the highly selective colleges do have an attrition rate and should be concerned with maximizing retention and graduation rates and meeting their mission and student academic and personal goals.

With this in mind, it is time to apply common sense to retention and graduation of students from colleges. Unfortunately, colleges are approaching the issue backward.

THIS IS IMPORTANT. Colleges look at student skills at entry, which is good, but they really do not know whether the skills match up with those required for a student to be successful in their foundation courses.

Foundation courses are the first college-level courses a student takes when she or he enters the college. For example, if the student is a business major, this may include introduction to business, composition, psychology, and others. A liberal arts major may include courses such as composition, introduction to the humanities, introduction to sociology, and others. Foundation courses are the first courses a student would take in their major provided she or he is college ready.

THE PRELIMINARIES

The key question is: What are the skills necessary for a student to be successful in her/his foundation courses? Not what are the skills a student brings with him/her to the college; that comes later. The skills a student brings with her/him does not matter much if the student's skills do not match the skills necessary to be successful in his/her foundation courses.

To determine the skills necessary for a student to be successful in her/his foundation courses, a college must first *assess their foundation courses prior to assessing the student.* Again, *assess your foundation courses prior to assessing the student.*

Questions that need to be answered during this foundation course evaluation process is: What is the reading level of the textbooks being used in foundation courses? Are the textbooks in foundations courses grade appropriate for a first-term college student? What writing skills are necessary to be successful in the foundation course, and do the courses include critical-thinking skills and mathematics?

Case in point. At a conference, the audience was asked if anyone knew the reading level of the textbook they were using in their courses. Not one audience member could answer that question. No one knew the reading level of the textbook they were using in their courses. The question, then, is how do they know that the textbook is reading-age appropriate and if the student is able to read and understand the textbook?

Another case in point. At another conference, one audience member stated that at his college, about 80 percent of the students in a college success course failed the course. The college success course is supposed to teach success skills and how to navigate the college system. When the college assessed the reading level of the course textbook they found it was on the master's level.

This prompted the college to adapt a new textbook that was reading-level appropriate for a first-year college student. About 80 percent of the students enrolled in the course after the textbook change passed the course. Obviously, if a student cannot understand the textbook due to its reading difficulty level, she or he will not be successful in the course.

Moral of the story? If you do not know the reading level of a textbook in your foundation courses or even beyond, you cannot assume it is age-level appropriate for your students. This also holds true for other skills that a student may need to know to be successful in a foundation course. For example, what are the writing skills needed for success in a foundation course? Is it important for a student to know noun/verb agreement? Will a student need the ability to read, synthesize, and write about what was read? Will a student have to write a paper in the course, and are they able to write a coherent paragraph? Are critical-thinking skills necessary to be successful in the foundation course? What mathematical skills are necessary to be successful in a foundation course?

Naturally these skills will vary from foundation course to foundation course, but there will be many commonalities. These commonalities could include appropriate reading level of text for a first-year college student, and the ability to analyze a paragraph or written paper and then synthesize and write an essay about the writing. This, of course, would entail critical-thinking skills. Is there any mathematics that a student would need in the foundation course (other than a mathematics major)?

There may very well be many skill areas that foundation courses have, or some that other foundation courses do not have. But in the end, there will be similar required skills that will surface and can be used and generalized for student success in a foundation course. So, assessment *must* begin with an evaluation of college foundation courses and the skills necessary for a student to be successful in them.

Once foundation courses' skill areas are determined and boiled down to the obvious few, such as reading, writing, critical thinking, and mathematics, you can *then* determine whether the student has the skills necessary to be successful in a foundation course. This is accomplished through assessment of the student's current skill knowledge.

But again, the assessment *must* take place *after* foundation courses have been identified and skills necessary in each one determined in reading, writing, critical thinking, and mathematics that will enable a student to be successful. *Only* after course assessment is completed can a student then be assessed to determine if she or he has the requisite skills to be successful in foundation courses or needs skill development prior to enrollment in foundation courses.

FIVE STEPS TO DETERMINE STUDENT COURSE PLACEMENT

Figure 11.1 below illustrates the process that a college should use to determine student course placement. Having a student skill level match those of foundations courses will ensure that the student is academically ready for those courses. *Note:* Step 4 in the retention process is the assessment of student skills.

This, of course, assumes that steps 1, 2, and 3 have been deployed: course skills have been identified and skill assessment is ready for the student to take. That is, once a student has been accepted to a college this process can begin. A college does not and should not wait until a student is on campus to begin the assessment of student's skills that were determined by the college for foundation courses.

Rather, it can begin at acceptance, in which a student can take the assessment over the web if desired by the college. Once course placement is deter-

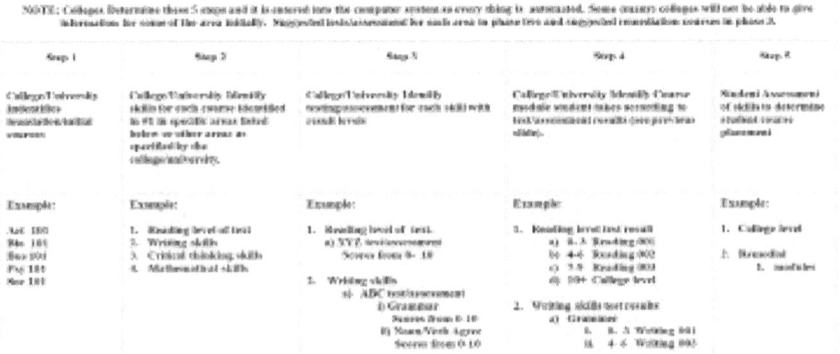

Figure 11.1. Five Steps to Determine Student Course Placement.
Seidman (2017).

mined, the student is enrolled in courses commensurate with her/his abilities. The entire process is explained in detail below.

STEPS TO IMPLEMENT
STUDENT COURSE PLACEMENT

The first thing a college needs to determine is student academic skill level and if it matches up with foundation course skills. The steps to implement proper course placement of students is quite simple. It assumes that academic preparation is paramount to be able to master college-level work. No matter how socially integrated a student is to the social aspects of a college, if she or he cannot read the text or write a paragraph she or he will not be successful.

So, let us get that out of the way for good and concentrate first and foremost on the academic aspects of student success. Later we will discuss how to socially integrate a student into the college experience.

This can be quite a powerful process: proper academic assessment, skill placement, and providing academic assistance as well as social integration. And always remember what Seidman says, *"Don't make it harder than it really is or needs to be."*

Step 1

Colleges (through their faculty) first need to identify foundation-level courses, all of them. These are the initial college-level courses a student would take in any program or major, assuming she or he is ready academically to take them. In other words, these are the first college-level courses a student would take in a major.

Examples of foundation level courses are: English 101, Psychology 101, Art 101, Foundations of Business Administration 101, Biology 101, Earth Science 101, and others. Foundation courses would be the courses a student with a college-level skill set would be enrolled in. Any course that a first-time student would take without a college course prerequisite can be considered a foundation course. These should be identified college wide; all programs and majors, all courses.

Step 2

For each foundation course that was identified in step 1, faculty need to identify the skills necessary for a student to be successful in the course (see figure 11.2). That is, what are the skills necessary for a student enrolled in

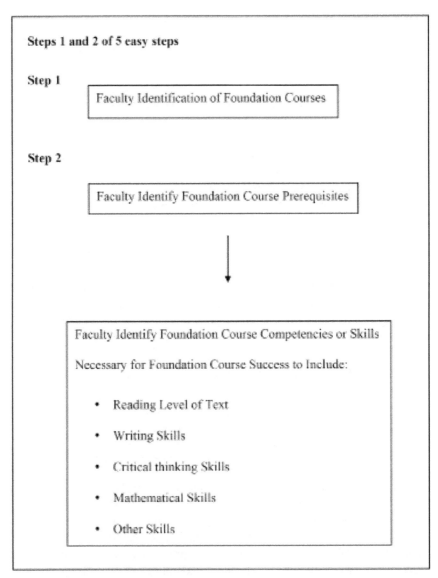

Figure 11.2.   Step 1 and 2 Illustration.
Seidman (2017).

the course to be able to successfully complete the course? Successful completion is defined as earning an A through C grade. Obviously, this assumes that
the student who meets the skill criteria through assessment completes the
assigned work and is not too socially integrated into the formal and informal
social systems and fails the course.

There should be some areas that are common to all foundation courses, such as the reading level of the textbook or other sourced reading material being at the first-year college level. Other sourced reading material can be supplemental articles and other materials that are assigned during the course.

Please note. If the reading material is greater than a college first level, then the reading material should be replaced by more appropriate reading-level material. *This is a key point.* If a student graduates from high school, it could be assumed that she or he has a twelfth-grade reading level and therefore is ready to continue her/his mastery of first-year college-level reading (or grade 13). If the textbook is greater than first-level college level it could be considered inappropriate for the student; that is, the student may have trouble with vocabulary and understanding concepts that are written "over her/his head."

Publishing companies should be able to provide the reading level of the textbooks they sell to colleges for all subjects. Pointed out earlier, a college success course was using a masters-level reading text. Eighty percent of the students failed the course. Once the textbook was changed to an age appropriate text, 80 percent of the students passed the course.

Textbook companies are in the business of selling books, so they should provide the college with the reading level of the textbooks they sell to your college. If they will not provide that information, then use another publisher who does provide the reading level of the textbook. In addition, if none of the textbooks of a publisher are at an age-appropriate level, ask the company to have the book rewritten by the author to ensure that the book is age appropriate for students.

Remember, again, textbook companies are in the business of selling textbooks and should do whatever they can to ensure that your college and others buy from them. Offering age-appropriate textbooks is a win-win for the college and textbook publisher.

Other common skill areas that should be identified could include: writing skills necessary for success (can be broken down to grammar, sentence structure, paragraph development, etc.), critical-thinking skills, and mathematical skills. This list is not all-inclusive, and colleges may want to add their own skills to the list. Remember, these skills should be geared for first-time college students; that is, the first year of college for foundation courses. What a college needs to do is to identify the most common foundation courses skills necessary for a student to be successful in those courses.

It should be noted that many skills may be identified through this process. That is a good thing. But common skill themes—that is, specific skills that are most common to all foundation courses—should supersede the many and be boiled down to a few; that is, the reading level of the text. If textbooks are at a greater level than a first-year college student's skills, then a textbook should be substituted for one at a first-year college student's expected reading level. That means that student assessment of reading level in step 3 needs only to identify students not ready for college-level reading.

Writing would be another area with subareas to be determined and assessed for each foundation course. Most college courses include a writing component (verb/noun agreement, sentence structure, paragraph development) that college faculty assume a recent high school graduate knows and expects to perform satisfactorily on written assignments.

Another common skill could also pertain to critical-thinking skills. These skills combined with reading proficiency and writing skills make for a powerful combination of skills necessary for students to be successful in all courses even beyond the first year.

Mathematics is another important skill not only for skill courses but also for college mathematics requirements. Many colleges expect a student to have specific knowledge of mathematics and to pass certain courses to graduate. So, this would appear to be a core foundation skill area along with reading, writing, and critical thinking.

Only the key skill areas that are common to most foundation courses should be identified and assessed up front. That means that these are the key skill areas that have been identified as important for student success in a foundation course. Consideration should also include a computer readiness assessment. Although we assume that students in this day and age are computer savvy, colleges may be surprised at how much students depend on the software to do its job and not know how to tweak programs or have control of programs.

Case in point. Most colleges use specific office programs that students are required to use throughout their college career. Being able to master Microsoft Word by setting specific font types and font size is important. Setting margins and spacing are important too. Knowing how to use track changes once a paper is returned is very helpful. These areas seem minor but are important. A quick computer assessment tool and follow-up noncredit quick course can really help students master common programs, which will save valuable time when using these programs for their courses.

There will be a few foundation courses that will fall outside of the standard skill areas. These could be art drawing, computer programing, and others. Students in very specialized programs with specialized foundation courses can be identified at the application stage. Supplemental assessment can be given to these students and specialized modules created to remediate any deficiencies.

Perhaps the first week of class these specialized skills can be assessed in class if they complement the standard skill areas to be assessed. It is important to note that a college should not overwhelm a student with assessment; rather, use assessment to help identify a student in need of skill help.

Over time, colleges will build enough data to demonstrate the worthiness of student skill assessment at entry. With this data, the college can demonstrate to reluctant students the merits of taking assessment and proper placement. Colleges should also review course requirements from time to time and assess students accordingly. Textbooks become outdated and need to be replaced. Keeping a concern for readability level is a key concept.

In step 1 the college has identified all college foundation courses. In step 2 the college has identified the skills necessary for a student to be successful in those identified foundation courses. There should be overlap in the skills necessary to be successful in foundation courses. In step 3 a college identifies the assessment necessary to determine the student's skill level at entry.

STEPS FOUR OF FIVE EASY STEPS: IDENTIFY ASSESSMENT FOR EACH SKILL WITH RESULT LEVELS

Steps 3 of 5 easy steps Identify Assessment for Each Skill with Result Levels

Example:

1. Reading Level of Students
   a) XYZ Test/Assessment
   Scores from 0–10
2. Writing Skills
   a) ABC Test/Assessment
   b) Grammar
   Scores from 0–10
   c) Noun/Verb Agree
   Scores from 0–10
3. Critical Thinking Skills
   a) DEF Test/Assessment
   Scores from 0–10
4. Mathematics
   a) GHI Test/Assessment
   Score Levels:
   i. Basic
   ii. Algebra
   iii. Geometry
   iv. College level

Step 3

Colleges need to determine which assessment tools will be used to measure the skills identified in step 2. Ideally the assessment should be a nationally normed assessment so there are no issues as to their reliability. It is much better to use already-in-existence assessment tools. There are many reputable test and measurement companies that can provide a comprehensive package of assessment tools to meet your college's needs.

Using locally developed assessments leaves the college open to accusations that they are using an unreliable assessment tool that does not measure what it is supposed to be measuring. This can occur until you record enough data to support your assessment efforts. There are on-campus experts and psychometricians who can assist with the task of choosing appropriate assessment tools. Assessment tools that have been used for years developed by major assessment companies ensures reliability and will back up college claims that assessment and placement actually help students.

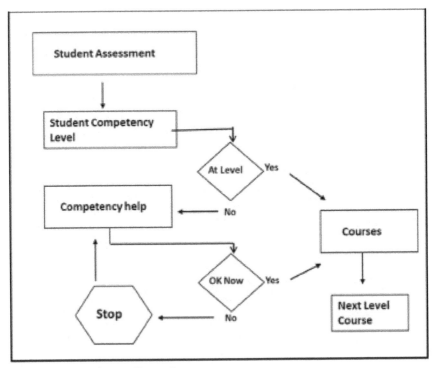

Figure 11.3.   Putting It All Together.
Seidman (2017).

Cut scores should be developed, which will determine whether a student meets college-level skill levels or needs to take skill-building remediation and which specific module(s) within the remediation. This will be discussed later. There are many well-recognized assessment/testing agencies that would be able to help a college decide on which assessment to use and cut scores for the various assessments.

Step 4

Once you have identified foundation courses, identified skills needed to be successful in each, and identified assessment with cut scores, student assessment, and placement comes next. Placing a student who meets the college-level criteria is easy. The student is enrolled into the college-level course and should be able to read the text, write a paper, critically think, and use mathematical skills.

But what about the student in need of remediation? The college needs to develop skill modules that correspond to assessment scores. For instance, if there are ten skills a student needs to know to be placed in college-level writing, then ten modules should be developed for each of the ten skills. In the past, if student #1 had five of ten skills she or he would be placed in a remedial course that started at skill one and had to work through all of the skills even if she or he knew some of them. The concept here, and as will be explained in the next chapter, is to provide only the deficient skills, not the ones the student already knows.

Step 5

Based on student assessment, she or he is placed into either college-level work, the first foundation courses, or placed into the proper remediation module(s).

Once all the steps are in place, students can take assessment directly after admissions acceptance and prior to enrollment. It should become part of the admissions acceptance and enrollment process. The student is then placed into the proper course(s) at either college level/ready or into specific remedial module(s).

Assessment should be given in a variety of modes. Accepted students should be able to take assessments over the web or on campus if appropriate, but as soon as possible after acceptance so course placement can be explained to the students and appeals heard. There always should be an appeals process in place, since no doubt a number of accepted students will not believe that they need remediation. Alternate versions of the assessment should be available. Appeals can be handled with on-campus supervised assessment to ensure honesty.

To eliminate the student having her/his PhD uncle take the web assessment, a pledge of authenticity should be signed. That is, the student signature signifies that the student pledges that she or he actually took the web assessment. If, later on, the student is not doing well in a foundation course, the assessment can be given again to confirm initial placement.

If it is determined that the student did not take the assessment, then that should be grounds for dismissal from the college. All colleges want students to succeed, and taking remediation is one way to do that. But if a student is dishonest and had someone else take the assessment, a college should not want a dishonest student enrolled in their college.

If a student assesses at a level that she or he needs remediation and the student refuses to accept the result, acceptance to the college should be withdrawn. Taking and abiding with the assessment results should be a part of the admissions acceptance criteria. If a student threatens to attend another college that would put the student into inappropriate college-level courses, let the student do so. Chances are very likely that the student will not be successful at that college and become an attrition statistic at that college.

Not many students want to enroll in non-college-credit-bearing remedial courses. But the choice will be evident. Taking the remedial modules will enable the student to gain the skills necessary to be successful in future college-level courses.

It must be stated here that a mechanism must be developed that tracks a students' progress throughout their college career. At the first sign of difficulty either academically or socially, the proper service areas should be contacted and an intervention initiated. This will be explained later. The next few pages will illustrate the five steps to assessment and placement.

To recap the five easy steps process: first and foremost, all foundation courses need to be identified. For the identified foundation courses, and really all courses (to be covered later), faculty need to identify prerequisites and skills competencies necessary to be successful in each course. Then identify assessment tools to assess student skills at entry. The assessment of student skills should take place prior to enrollment.

If specific skills are needed, then the student is enrolled in the remediation skill models depending on the skill deficiency. Once the skill(s) is acquired the student can then be placed into the proper college-level course. The underlying assumption is that the student needs specific skills to be successful in foundational courses. Once the skill(s) is successfully demonstrated by the student, she or he can be placed into the college-level courses.

The process needs to be a partnership involving all constituent groups of the college; that is, faculty and offices that assess student needs, discuss student course placement and other issues. The primary objective should be to make sure that the college or university is true to its mission and that students understand the mission and are properly prepared to meet the challenges associated with courses necessary to achieve their individual academic and personal goals.

Once the faculty have selected prerequisites and determined skills necessary to be successful in a course, the college or university can assess an accepted student to determine whether or not she or he needs to take any remediation modules. The assessment of student skills can be taken over the web or at the institution. Whenever or wherever the assessment is given, the student would sign of pledge of authenticity. The pledge of authenticity indicates that it is indeed the student taking the assessment. Within the process, if the pledge of authenticity is broken, then the student is subject to disciplinary measures that would include dismissal from the college.

Directly after assessment, assuming it is web based, the competency level of the student is determined and the student placed accordingly in either college-level courses or remediation modules. This can include automatic placement or the student meeting with an advisor directly after the assessment in person or over the web face to face or by phone. If the assessment is taken on campus, the meeting with an advisor for the student's intended major can take place immediately, where an explanation of the placement is given.

In addition, at this time a mini-orientation can be given to the student explaining college resources and other items. For those students taking the assessment over the web, the student can then schedule a phone or web-based meeting with an advisor who would interpret the assessment results and place the student accordingly. Naturally, an appeal process can be instituted as necessary, and the number of times a student can retake the assessment should be established.

This process should become part of the admissions process. It should be mandatory if the student wants to enroll at the college. If a student refuses to take the assessment or abide by the results, then the college does not have to accept the student (this includes open admissions institutions) since the student is not abiding by the college criteria for admittance to the college. Remember, if the student is misplaced due to not taking the assessment or wants to enroll in a college-level class even though the assessment says otherwise, chances are that the student will not be successful and become an attrition statistic.

If the student meets the appropriate competency level, the student is placed in the college-level course. Later on we will look at the faculty role in ensuring that the student is placed properly even after assessment. This is an important part of the process. Faculty know their students better than we like to give them credit. Ask any faculty member after the first week of class and they will tell you which students will have problems completing the course successfully.

Therefore, a student check-up with faculty the first week of class is a way to ensure proper placement and student success. If through this system students are placed properly, you will have a very happy and satisfied faculty. No more complaints from faculty having underprepared students in their classes or having to dilute the course.

The college wins by providing programs and services for students that are accepted. Placing a student properly into courses will enable the student to obtain their academic and personal goals. The student will stay enrolled through goal attainment, most likely meaning through graduation. College retention term to term and graduation rates will go up.

Key ideas of this chapter were the Seidman Student Success Formula/ Model and Five Steps to Success. The five easy steps were: the identification of foundation courses, identification of foundation course skills necessary for a student to be successful, choosing assessment tools, developing cut scores for assessment, and placing students into proper courses using assessment.

Chapter Twelve

Need for Skill Development

Now that the identification of a student in need of skill development has been discussed, it is time to turn attention to how to provide and deliver skill-development courses to students in need. Writing will be used to illustrate the skill-building process, but this could also apply to reading, critical thinking, mathematics, and more.

For discussion purposes, let us say that the faculty have identified six major writing skills they deem necessary for a student to be successful in foundation courses. Naturally, some foundation courses may identify more or less skills, but for argument's sake and illustration purposes, let us say that the consensus of the faculty are that there are six writing skills that are necessary for student success. Since there may be other writing skills identified by faculty for other foundation courses, it is best to use the most common for skill-development modules that will be discussed later in this chapter. Figure 12.1 illustrates the current student placement in a skills-development course.

Using figure 12.1, student #1 is deficient in two of the six skills identified by faculty in writing after taking the writing assessment. Student #2 is deficient in four of the six skills identified by faculty in writing after taking the writing assessment.

Please note. The writing assessment does not take into account faculty-identified writing skills. The assessment is a tool that the college hopes will cover skill deficiencies.

Currently, regardless of the number of skill competency deficiencies a student has, both students are placed in the same skill-development course. It does not matter if the student needs only two or four skills. The students, regardless of the skills needed, are placed into the beginning of a remedial writing course and must stay in it all term.

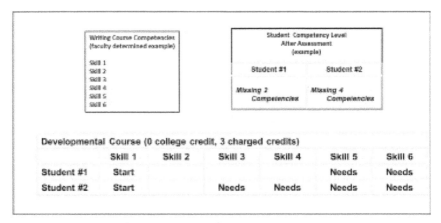

Figure 12.1. Current Skill Placement Model.
Seidman (2017).

Additionally, current writing courses are hit and miss. That is, since skill competencies have not been identified by the faculty for foundation courses, some of the skills necessary for success may not even be taught in the remedial course. Therefore, it is imperative for a college to have faculty identify the skills necessary for student success in foundation courses and develop modules that cover each skill. It cannot be assumed that your remedial courses will teach the skills necessary for student success if you have not examined each course and developed a list of the skills necessary for success.

In the current model of student remedial placement, both students start at the beginning of the course and may already know the material. It may take until midterm or end of the term for the course to cover the material that the students actually need, or maybe not at all if the faculty have not designated what writing skills are needed for success.

It is no wonder that students complain about their placement in remedial courses. The skill deficiency may not be covered until the last part of the course; therefore, the student may complain that she or he already knows the material, so why is she or he being placed into a remedial course in the first place.

Additionally, remedial courses usually do not count for college credit since they are not considered college level. So, the student complains that she or he is being charged for a course that she or he does not need and is not being given college credit either. This causes many student complaints whether it is justified or not. Students have a valid complaint if she or he is not receiving the requisite skills until the later part of a course or at all. Students should receive the skills they need immediately. Figure 12.2 shows how this can happen.

So, what can be done? In this example, there were six writing skills identified by faculty as being essential for student success in college foundation courses. So why not develop modules for each of the six writing skills? The modules can be of varying length depending on the nature of the skill needing to be learned by the student.

A compilation of all six skills could span one or more terms depending on the mastery of each. If a student works on a skill at her/his own pace, then much can be accomplished. Similar to regular classes, writing remedial students should meet with faculty members a minimum of three hours per week or more. A student can be required to complete two modules a term to be in good standing.

Figure 12.2 shows the proper student placement in skill-development modules. Students should only have to take the competencies or skills in which they are deficient. In other words, if a student is deficient in four writing skills and another student is deficient in two, then the first student should be required to take four skill modules while the other student needs to take two skill modules. In essence, each skill should be offered in modules that build upon each other; for example, sentence structure comes before paragraph construction, and more.

As mentioned earlier, a specific time to complete skills, such as a minimum of two modules per term, should be employed, and failure to complete the modules would have academic consequences. Naturally there should be some sort of time limit to complete skills, or the student can be deemed as not having the Ability to Benefit (ATB) from the education provided at the college.

Student Placement into Modules

Writing Course Competencies (faculty determined example)	Student Competency Level After Assessment (example)	
	Student #1	Student #2
Skill 1		
Skill 2		
Skill 3		
Skill 4	Missing 2	Missing 4
Skill 5	Competencies	Competencies
Skill 6		

Developmental Course (0 college credit, 3 charged credits)

	Skill 1	Skill 2	Skill 3	Skill 4	Skill 5	Skill 6
Student #1	X	X	X	X	Start	Needs
Student #2	X	X	Start	Needs	Needs	Needs

Figure 12.2. Proper Student Placement.
Seidman (2017).

A WORD ABOUT ABILITY TO BENEFIT (ATB)

So, what exactly is the concept of Ability to Benefit (ATB)? This concept can be applied to all students whether wanting to take courses at a community college or a four-year college. Most, if not all, states have this designation.

If a student cannot benefit from the educational experience (demonstrated by assessment and/or not completing remedial modules after numerous tries), then a college does not have to accept the student or allow her/him to continue at the college. In the case of assessment and placement of a student into specific remedial modules, after a specific period of time if the student cannot complete the modules, then she or he can be declared not ATB and released from the college or university.

A student should not be counted as a student for any purpose until they complete remediation and enroll in college-level courses. Remedial courses can be offered at a deep tuition discount if financial aid will not cover the cost. The discounted tuition for remedial modules will be recouped many times over as the student will acquire the skills necessary to be successful and stay at the college until academic and personal goal attainment, which usually means graduation instead of dropping out after one or two terms.

Naturally these students should not be counted in the retention/attrition statistics. But again, this is where the mission of a college comes into play. If the mission is to take in marginal students and try to provide programs and services to help the student succeed, then longer attempts to successfully complete remedial modules is in order.

It is up to the college to determine the length of time to complete a module. What to call your remediation program? How about a Skills Academy? You can charge half the cost of regular tuition or charge by the module.

AN EXAMPLE OF MODULE
REMEDIATION OR SKILLS ACADEMY

There is precedence for modular remediation. Foothill College in California redeveloped its remedial math program from courses to modules in an effort to improve mathematics retention and completion (most of this section is taken from Silverman and Seidman 2011–2012). California has a requirement that a student must successfully complete two college math courses (Math 101, Beginning Algebra, and Math 105, Intermediate Algebra) to graduate from a community college. Foothill College developed a modular math sequence called Math My Way (MMW).

Table 12.1 shows the previous math sequence prior to MMW. In the previous math sequence, if the student assessed at the lowest-level course the

Table 12.1. Previous Math Sequence at Foothill College

Math 250	Arithmetic
Math 200	Pre-algebra
Math 101	Beginning Algebra
Math 105	Intermediate Algebra

student was enrolled in Math 250, arithmetic. The student had one quarter to complete the course. The faculty controlled the pacing of the course. It met for five hours per week. There was a thirty-five-to-one student-faculty ratio. The failure rate was high.

Table 12.2 shows the MMW sequence of courses. The new course, Math 230, is divided into ten hierarchical and sequential modules. A student is placed into a module based on assessment scores. For instance, a student may be placed into module 3 and would have to complete modules three through ten to complete the course and thus move into Math 101, Beginning Algebra.

This is a mastery learning of concepts in which a module builds upon another. That is, the student needs to master module 1 prior to taking module 2, and so on. Whereas in the old sequence of remedial math the faculty controlled the pacing of the course, MMW has flexible pacing and is student controlled. Students meet with faculty for ten hours per week with a 150-to-5 student-faculty ratio. To continue in the course, a student must complete at least two modules per term.

In addition, there is a spiraling assessment in which a student must receive 100 percent on all assignments or she or he must retake the concept and redo the assignment until she or he receives 100 percent on the assignments. To move from one module to the next, a student must receive a score of 87 percent. In addition to the five faculty working with the approximately 150 students, peer tutors are also employed for assistance.

The study by Silverman and Seidman (2011–2012) of MMW versus the old math sequence showed MMW students demonstrated significant program progression through the math sequence. In addition, MMW students had significantly higher math GPAs than the old math sequence. There were other possible consequences of taking MMW versus the old sequence. This

Table 12.2. MMW Sequence of Courses at Foothill College

Math 230 (new course)	MMW: Arithmetic + Pre-algebra
Math 101	Beginning Algebra
Math 105	Intermediate Algebra

includes more basic-skills students (minorities, women, nontraditional) completing academic requirements.

Does the system work? One student began at the second-grade level in math and reached college level in two years. Students who complete all college mathematics requirements may increase career aspirations. Also, it was demonstrated that more students were turned on to math. Finally, the college increased revenue by keeping students through academic and personal goal completion and thus meeting its mission.

Key points of this chapter reviewed the process of providing needed skills for students in progressive modules. Foothill College MMW was used as an example of how a modular approach to remediation can work (the information regarding MMW came from Silverman and Seidman, 2011–2012). Giving a student only the skills she or he is deficient in just makes sense instead of putting a student into a full-term class that may or may not cover student deficiencies. Using the modular method can allow a student to complete deficiencies midterm or earlier. When that happens, a college can give supplemental work in preparation for the student entering the college-level course the following term.

The proceeding involved the preassessment of student skills and how to remediate deficiencies. We now turn our attention to monitoring a student once enrolled.

Chapter Thirteen

Moving beyond Assessment and Initial Placement

The Seidman Student Success Model

Once a student has been assessed and placed properly into courses, there is much that can be done throughout the student's college career to help her/him achieve her/his academic and personal goals. Short of RFIDing a student to determine where a student is at all times (parents may like this idea), colleges can provide programs and services to help the student through an often complicated educational process. Colleges need to be proactive and make contact with their students on a continual basis prior to enrollment and through the student's college career. Figure 13.1 illustrates this process and will be discussed in length.

Figure 13.1 shows how the Seidman retention formula—Retention = Early $_{\text{ID}}$ + (Early + Intensive + Continuous)$_{\text{IV}}$—fits in with the Seidman Student Success Model. Much time has been devoted to Early Identification through assessment. Now we discuss how to provide Early + Intensive + Continuous Intervention for students throughout their college career.

The formula starts with the premise that the student comes first. The teaching-learning process is essential for student academic and personal growth and development. A student enters the institution to acquire academic and personal skills necessary to achieve academic and personal goals.

Assessment and interventions are a longitudinal process commencing at the time of acceptance and continuing throughout the student's career at the institution and perhaps beyond. Although the formula appears to be for one term, it is, in essence, for all terms a student is enrolled at the institution and perhaps beyond.

There are three paths a student can take after assessment and initial placement, the keystone of the process. These three paths include: ready for college-level work; the need for skill building or remediation, or a combination of the two; remediation for some areas such as mathematics and placement

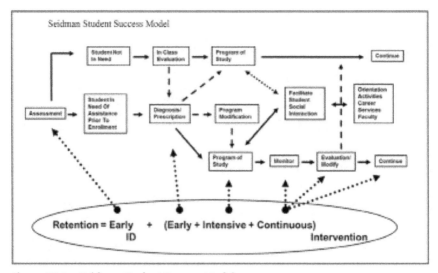

Figure 13.1.   Seidman Student Success Model.
Seidman (2003).

into college level courses. A student can need mathematics skill building but be ready for college-level reading and writing. So, a student can be enrolled in college-level foundation courses that do not require college-level mathematics.

We have pretty much covered the student that needs remediation. The thought here is to give the student the necessary skills to be successful and to place her/him into college-level foundation courses as soon as practical. That is directly after the successful completion of skill acquisition though taking modules in the areas of deficiencies. Remember, the identification of skills necessary to be successful in foundation courses is essential and comes first prior to student assessment.

STUDENT IN NEED OF SKILL
BUILDING (REMEDIATION)

Following the Seidman Success Model path, the student in need of skill building after assessment is placed into a program of study (lower part of model). It is perhaps most beneficial, if after assessment, that a student meets with an advisor to review and discuss assessment results and plan with the student first-term modules/courses to enroll in. This is important for the student to fully understand the preenrollment assessment process and the consequences of the results.

The student will probably look at remediation as a failure, but the advisor can turn student negativity into a positive by pointing out that the successful completion of remediation will equip the student to be successful in college-level courses. Once enough data is gathered to show the positive results of remediation, the student and her/his parents will see the wisdom of the placement process and may even embrace it.

A student's progress should be continually monitored, and upon evaluation of progress throughout the term a student would either stay in skill-building modules or, if completed, have their program modified and moved to the top part of the model and enroll in college-level courses. All student progress and contact should be computerized and systemized, and notification of meetings are sent to students, faculty, and appropriate staff who will interact with the student. Continued personalized contact with a student will enable the building of trust and ease the student into the proper course of enrollment action.

It should be noted that while enrolled in skill-building modules, or for that matter college-level courses, there is a facilitation of social interactions to be discussed later.

STUDENT ASSESSMENT INTO COLLEGE-LEVEL COURSES

Although a student may be assessed at college-level work, it would behoove a college to also use faculty knowledge of student behaviors in class to assist in the process. Colleges do not use faculty knowledge of student behaviors as much as they should. If a college dean went into a veteran faculty member's classroom the first week of class and asked the faculty member which students she or he thinks will be unsuccessful, the dean would be surprised to receive an accurate answer.

All faculty need to assess student course readiness (backing up the assessment) the first few days of the term. This can be an in-class assessment assignment, or it can be an assignment due the next class session. Faculty can then assess the assignment to make sure that the student is placed properly. In addition, if a student does not complete the assignment in class or has the assignment for the next class, there may be an issue with time management and other issues. An intervention with the student should commence right away.

There also needs to be a mechanism in place whereby faculty can identify a student who she or he feels will need either academic or social support and report it immediately. The obvious method would be for faculty to report a student immediately through email to a specific office, which would parse the email and route it to the proper office and person who will contact the faculty member and/or student right away.

Colleges need to marshal all of their services the first two weeks of the term to make sure that students are placed appropriately and that responses to faculty concerns are addressed immediately. Colleges need to be flexible enough to be able to meet with a student and nimble enough to move a student into the proper path (ready for college-level courses, skill building, or both) the first two weeks of the term. Initial and proper course placement is key to student success.

This means there must be a strong connection between faculty, administration, staff, and support systems such as counseling and advising. If a college is lucky enough to have a well-staffed counseling and or advising center, then faculty should contact this office to intervene with a student immediately. The student should be contacted and meet with the counselor or advisor to discuss the faculty observation and be placed into proper courses. The college needs to be flexible enough to move students into appropriate courses the first few weeks of the term.

If faculty serve as advisors, then they need to be available to meet with students in lieu of the counseling and/or advising staff. Faculty need to be available and reachable to meet with students. If this means that faculty need to be on campus and available from 8 a.m. to 8 p.m. for the first two weeks, then that has to be put into faculty contracts to ensure that this important function is carried out. Colleges will have to decide which faculty functions are valued—teaching, advising, service, publishing. If students truly come first, then faculty involvement with students inside and outside the classroom should take priority.

Faculty interaction with students inside and outside the classroom must be valued by the college in faculty tenure and promotion decisions. Colleges must stay true to their missions and support faculty who help make that mission possible. Publishing is great for faculty, college visibility, and prestige, but helping a student achieve her/his academic and personal goals is the greater good and the better contribution to our society. If necessary, give faculty lighter course loads so she or he can advise students regularly and have time to produce research articles. Colleges can even differentiate faculty into practitioners and researchers, adapting faculty loads accordingly.

It is true that some faculty are just not good at advising or do not care to do it. That should not be considered a negative. Instead, a college should want only the best faculty to advise students if that is the college's model of advising. Naturally, faculty who want to advise students should go through thorough training. Those that rather not advise should have publishing, service, and the like paramount in the promotion and tenure process.

Deans of the faculty must be actively involved with continually monitoring and observing faculty to ensure that quality teaching and advising is occurring. Standards for faculty teaching effectiveness must be developed and followed. Evaluation should not be punitive but rather prescriptive, where faculty can grow in their positions over the years. Offices of Faculty Excellence and similar programs are excellent avenues for this.

The research is clear that faculty interaction with students outside the formal classroom setting is important for student success. So how can a college encourage and promote faculty-student interaction? Colleges need to realize that faculty have competing interests: research, publishing, committees. Promotions and tenure are dependent on these.

If a faculty member needs to return a revised manuscript for publication by Friday and it is Wednesday, you can best bet where the faculty member's priority will be—meeting with students or working on the manuscript? Colleges need to value faculty involvement with students in the evaluation and promotion process.

Faculty should also be encouraged to meet with students by going to the student union or library to meet informally with them. Faculty would be amazed that students do not really equate them as parents, brothers, and sisters. Students seem to hold faculty to a higher standard or level due to their educational attainment. Sitting with a group of students in the student union over coffee enables students to see that a faculty member is a real person with similar issues that their parents have, and they can talk about the experiences they are having as a first-term college student.

Key points in this chapter reviewed the Seidman Student Success Model and how the Seidman retention formula fits into the model. Also discussed was how student assessment of skills fits into the model. Now we will turn our attention to how colleges can help faculty excel in the teaching process. Chapter 15 will discuss student social integration into the college that is a part of the Seidman Student Success Model.

Chapter Fourteen

Faculty Teaching Practice

Faculty are key to helping a student achieve her/his academic and personal goals and helping a college meet its mission. But unfortunately, some of our faculty need to hone their teaching skills to become even more effective teachers. Many colleges forget that faculty are not trained to be teachers; rather, they are experts in their chosen field. For the most part, they do not have to be certified, pass any tests, and once they receive tenure they are usually not observed by the administration for teaching effectiveness.

Elementary, secondary, special education—nearly all teachers as part of their college curriculum take methods courses in language arts, mathematics, science, social studies, and other subjects as appropriate. Although it is not obvious, there are different methods to teaching those subjects. Simply being an expert in a field does not guarantee ability to teach.

College faculty do not have to take methods courses or develop behavioral objectives; what behavioral value would a student gain from the lesson plan for each class day. Methods of teaching, behavioral objectives, and knowledge of different learning styles are essential for material presentation in the classroom.

Teaching faculty different methods of teaching their subject areas and development of behavioral objectives and learning styles can be a powerful tool for faculty presentations in the classroom and student learning. Do faculty know what teaching practices and/or methodologies can be used to accommodate different student learning styles?

There are different types of learners in the classroom, and one teaching method or style does not work for all students. Do faculty know the basic techniques to teach or even identify different types of learners, such as the visual learner, verbal learner, tactile learner, group learner, individual learner?

Can a student have more than one learning style? Of course. Should faculty use different learning style techniques in the classroom? Of course.

Do faculty use different classroom practices that can try to accommodate students with different learning styles, such as group work, individual work, or combination group/individual work or different lecture techniques? Do they use the chalkboard or MSPPTs for the visual learner and voice presentations for the verbal leaner?

Are faculty available before and after class to meet with students to clarify class content? Are office hours flexible so students can seek out faculty at off hours? Do faculty teach and run directly after class?

Many colleges have Centers for Teaching Excellence or similarly named Centers. These Centers usually offer seminars and webinars on specific topics such as research funding availability. Few offer teaching techniques, and if they do attendance is voluntary. Colleges need to teach faculty methods of student learning. They need to know what teaching practices and/or methodologies can be used to accommodate different student learning styles—the visual learner, verbal learner, tactile learner, group learner, and individual leaner.

Faculty need to know how to integrate them into their classrooms through group work, individual work, combination group/individual work, visual and verbal, and be available to help students where necessary. Not all methods are conducive to all subject matter, but knowledge of different ways to present knowledge in the classroom can only enhance the student learning experience.

These programs and webinars and in-person services to help faculty become better teachers should be mandatory for all new hires during faculty orientation and during at least the first year. Every three years those who went through the initial teaching practices and/or methodologies that can be used to accommodate different student learning styles should take a refresher. Department heads need to observe faculty regularly to ensure that these proven techniques are being used. This is similar to colleges having faculty take FERPA and harassment seminars regularly.

Since the goal is to meet the college mission of educating students for specific careers or lifelong learning, it is imperative that we provide faculty with the tools to do just that. Stated earlier, the money spent up front to fund these types of faculty centers of excellence and their programs will be returned many times over as students meet their academic and personal goals. Students will thrive and stay at an institution that really cares about their personal growth and development. Satisfied students stay to graduate and tell their friends about the education they received.

Key points of this chapter touched upon what faculty and colleges can do to enhance their teaching. The next chapter reviews ways college can help facilitate student social integration. Though not as important as academic integration, coupled together it makes for a powerful combination to help students accomplish their academic and personal goals and help colleges meet their individual mission.

Chapter Fifteen

Facilitating Student Social Interaction

The Seidman Student Success Model (see figure 13.1) has built in a student social interaction with the formal and informal social systems of a college. Although social integration into the formal and informal systems of a college (see Tinto, 1993) is important, it is not as important as academic integration into the formal and informal systems, but it should not be overlooked. The two in combination can make for a powerful retention system.

Naturally if a student is not ready for college-level work and is placed incorrectly into courses, she or he will not be successful. Conversely, if a student is so integrated into the social systems of a college she or he may not complete coursework and not be retained. There needs to be a balance between academics and the social aspects of college.

There are many in and out of class activities that faculty and others can lead that would help students succeed and feel a part of the college socially and in particular in their academic area of interest. What follows is a list of some of those activities with descriptions. This is not all-inclusive, and colleges can provide students with additional social events.

Faculty can announce these events in class and encourage students to attend. If the activity is curriculum related, perhaps extra credit can be given for attending the event or faculty discussing the event either in the classroom or informally after the event took place.

Most colleges have many activities that students can attend throughout each term. These include sporting events both varsity and intramural, concerts, plays, art exhibits, lectures, and more. Most often these events are advertised on bulletin boards in visible locations, but otherwise it is up to the student to see them and decide to attend them. It would be best if coaches, conductors, and those who actually take part in the event invite their fellow students to attend.

This can be accomplished by using the first few minutes of a class to give students the opportunity to invite classmates to events that they are participating in or helped organize. Student to student is usually more effective than faculty to student. Also, if faculty attended some of the events it would demonstrate to students their value. Faculty can also bring family or friends to these events.

There are other types of activities that can get students to participate and take advantage of to help them become integrated into the social systems of a college. One of these are curriculum clubs. Curriculum clubs are where students in similar programs, from first year through fourth year, can gather to talk about curriculum-specific topics and issues.

Even those interested in another curriculum can be urged to attend so they can get a feel for the program and field of study in case they want to change majors. The data is clear that a student who is undecided on a potential career choice has a high likelihood of leaving a college prematurely.

During these curriculum club meetings, action on specific items that affect the campus, state, or nation can be planned. Talk is nice, but action is better; applying what is learned to real campus, state, or national issues demonstrates the importance of the potential career. Additionally, opposing sides can be taken on issues, and debates on their merits can take place. This provides an avenue for real social change and teaches students how to go about trying to make social change in a proper fashion.

Food almost always draws people together. A curriculum or specialty interest group meeting without food just might not cut it with the masses! Therefore, another type of social event can be a coffee/tea/pizza event held once a month or more frequently. This can help bond students to students, upper second-, third-, and fourth-year students with first-year students.

Again, this can be by curriculum clubs or by special interests. This can also demonstrate faculty interest and involvement with their students. Any time faculty meet with students outside of the formal classroom is a plus. Students see faculty as real people, and it indicates that she or he is truly interested in student growth and development.

Lectures on and off campus (perhaps for extra credit) can be an effective way to involve students in other-than-academic programs and promote social integration to the college. Also invite or have current faculty give lectures in their research field or hobby interest areas. It is amazing the diverse types of research that faculty conduct, and student interest in those endeavors can be high. In fact, this might even lead to faculty-student collaboration on future research. Faculty talking about hobbies and the like can also match similar interests with students.

Students should also be encouraged to attend specific off-campus lectures. Perhaps extra credit can be given with verification of attendance by way of a one-page summary of the event. Naturally, the lecture should be a reasonable distance from campus. Also attending a campus lecture in other than one's own field should be encouraged. Diversity of thought is one of the cornerstones of our higher educational system.

Another social activity for students can be service learning and/or community service, perhaps again for extra credit. But most important is to include as part of the curriculum or final student class or project some kind of community service related to their curriculum or major. Attending college for two to four years earning an associates or bachelor's degree teaches students a lot in a specific area.

Students can use this knowledge to develop or participate in a related community service project either at the college campus for those living away from home or in the home community. This can instill the concept of giving back to the community. Many high schools are requiring a community service component to earn a high school diploma. Colleges should require this type of project too.

Early immersion in the curriculum is another way to help students see what the challenges and benefits of a particular major entail. This can occur prior to enrollment as part of the admission process, particularly in the health sciences, but it can be required for any area. A student who wants to enroll in a specific major can arrange to meet with a person in their community in the same area to discuss the educational requirements of the major and career path.

This can help the student to clarify career goals. A one-page essay can be required to demonstrate that the student took part in the activities. The essay can also be used to evaluate student writing readiness.

Case in point. At a conference luncheon, a table of nurses lamented the dropout rate after the students attended their first hospital clinical experience. It seemed that many students had a different reality of what duties a nurse preformed. It was suggested to the nurses that perhaps prior to admittance into the nursing program that a student shadow a nurse for a day so she or he can see the demands of the job.

The nurses indicated that could occur and that they had alums throughout the state that they were sure would participate in that type of student experience. In addition, providing alums with certificates of appreciation to hang on their office or work areas was also suggested. Everyone likes to hang certificates for all to see their contribution to their field. Whether this activity was actually implemented, and its outcomes measured, was not available.

Another case in point. This retention-of-nurses situation reminds of teacher training programs. Similarly, the real first encounter with students usually takes place for one term during the third-year practicum and fourth-year student teaching experiences. Once out in the field, some students quickly change their minds about teaching and then change their major.

Two-plus years of education in the wrong major most likely contributed to a longer stay at the college (more money) and perhaps attrition. The sooner a student can go out into the field and see what the major entails is a plus. Again, having as part of the admissions process a student spending a day with a person in their area of interest can only help a student clarify career goals.

Faculty in specific majors can invite alums to come into classrooms or assemblies to talk about their careers and how the curriculum contributed to their success. This gives students a real-life example of successful alums in the major they are enrolled in and pursuing. Naturally, having both genders invited to speak is preferable so all students can see the benefits of the major. Give alums a certificate of appreciation for their time and effort. Everyone likes to hang a certificate of appreciation on their office wall.

In addition, all colleges should have a study of the graduates that indicate the percentage of students who enrolled in specific majors, graduated within six years, got jobs in the field, and their starting salary. This should be given to all students in all majors at the start of their college careers and followed up on each year. In essence, it tells students the cost benefit of attending the college and enrolling in a specific major.

Another way to engage faculty and students is through discussion groups. Faculty can take turns holding weekly or bimonthly discussion groups on specific curriculum topics in person and/or on the web. Topics can vary about the fundamental issues of the day that relate to the major and curriculum either locally, statewide, or nationally. Giving students the opportunity to discuss current curriculum issues makes the area very relevant.

Internships are another way to immerse students into a program or major. Curriculum internships are a wonderful way to get students into the field early to really see what it is like to work in a particular field. These could be paid or unpaid, and the possible relationship building for when a student graduates can be immeasurable. Many firms may like to hire those they know and trust and have been employed through paid or unpaid internships.

The education student teaching model and graduate business and law model serve as prime examples of this type of activity. During student teaching, relationships are developed with a particular school. If a job in the students' area should become available for the following year, most would rather hire someone they know versus those they do not know. Oftentimes law firms hire summer student interns. This is a great way to learn and demonstrate ability, so when an opening occurs at the law firm the intern is high on the hiring list.

A curriculum newsletter edited by students and faculty is another way to engage students in their major. The curriculum newsletter can be published monthly, edited by students and faculty, and emailed to students or posted online. Sending a newsletter during the summer can really hold student interest and encourage early enrollment for the upcoming term. A summer newsletter can also give the student enrollment information, announce new course offerings, and introduce new faculty.

Today most students use social media to interact with each other. Developing a social media site restricted to students at your college in specific curriculums for communications purposes can be a powerful tool. This is especially true when the college is not in session between terms and particularly during the summer break.

Keeping students engaged during these down times can keep student interest in the college and major high. Also, if a faculty member sees an inappropriate or inaccurate post, she or he can respond to it immediately, setting the record straight or initiating a discussion that can carry over to the upcoming term.

Colleges can develop an overall college newsletter. These newsletters can be paper and/or email or social media to all students, new or continuing. Sending one between terms and one or two during the summer can help keep student interest and provide valuable information for the upcoming terms. For the new student, this can heighten the excitement of attending college and get the student to complete any requested and required items such as assessment and financial aid forms.

Key points of this chapter reviewed a few activities that a college can use to help keep students engaged with their curriculum and the college in general. Not only is academic integration important, but student social integration is as well. Although not as important as academic integration, social integration coupled with academic integration can be a powerful tool for student success. The following chapter will review other campus programs and services that can help students achieve their academic and personal goals.

Chapter Sixteen

A Word About . . .

Without teaching faculty there is no college. A college can exist without student services, but not without faculty. That said, there are many important student support services that contribute to student success. Often these offices are not given the respect or assistance necessary to carry out their function effectively and efficiently. They also tend to take a lot of criticism from the college community. Most are staffed by nonacademics without doctorates and may be looked down upon by the teaching faculty and administration. Many do not generate revenue and are therefore looked upon as a luxury.

Educational institutions are highly credentialed organisms, and sometimes they do not give enough attention to those who are not as highly credentialed as faculty. Sometimes student services are seen as necessary, but it takes money from the teaching function. Yet without them many students would be unable to attend college, or stay for that matter.

Below are some of those offices, their functions, and importance to the college. What is missing and not attended to by the college is also explored. Suggestions are given. This is not an exhaustive list, and many colleges have many more valuable student services.

Unfortunately, some colleges judge programs and services by the revenue they generate. But not counted by supposed nongenerating-revenue student services is if they did not exist perhaps more students would leave the college prematurely, losing the college revenue. So for every student that student services helps and stays enrolled in the college, the more revenue that is generated.

ACADEMIC AND STUDENT SERVICES

There are many different organizational patterns associated with these two areas. Usually the largest is Academic Affairs or Services, which include all teaching faculty and programs. The Office of Student Affairs or Services is usually headed by a vice president, provost, or dean who reports to the president of the college and serves on the president's council. With this organizational pattern the vice presidents of Academic and Student Affairs are supposed to be equal since they both report to the president and both serve on the president's council or cabinet.

In reality, a college can exist without a Student Affairs office, but not without faculty. In actuality, the Academic Affairs budget takes up a much larger portion of the college budget than Student Affairs. Most of Academic Affairs personnel have terminal degrees, whereas Student Affairs personnel usually do not. Academic Affairs generate revenue, and except for the Financial Aid Office, which may or may not be in the Student Affairs area, it does not generate revenue or very little.

Even colleges that have an organizational pattern of one vice president for both areas, Academic Affairs usually has priority over Student Affairs in budgeting, programming, and authority. With this dichotomy, academic and student areas are not equal. Except for the president's council, which may meet once a month or less, Academic Affairs assets more power and prestige than Student Affairs.

Julius Ford, retired vice president at Westchester Community College, used to say, "Student Affairs is the glue that holds the college together." In essence, he is correct. Without Student Affairs, social integration would not occur and students in need of assistance from a counseling and advising standpoint would not receive its benefits and perhaps leave the college prematurely.

What can be done to try to meld these diverse but critical areas together? Since they both usually have separate councils—the vice president of Academic Affairs has bimonthly meetings with area deans and the vice president of Student Affairs has bimonthly meetings with directors—why not hold a joint meeting every other month to share concerns and ideas?

Why not have an Academic Affairs council member serve on the Student Affairs counsel and vice versa? With vast insights into the workings of each major college area, Academic and Student Affairs can only enhance the understanding of each area and further the learning experience of students.

ORIENTATION PROGRAMS

Orientation programs are an important aspect for colleges that help students adjust and parents to understand the differences their son or daughter will encounter between the high school and college experience. Most colleges have online or in-person orientation programs for students. Online orientation is usually provided by community colleges and open admission institutions that take students up to the beginning of a term. These types of colleges often do not have the luxury of forming a class a few months before the start of a term.

If a college has an in-person orientation and a student misses it for a variety of reasons, an online orientation should be developed and be mandatory that a student complete the various modules prior to attending the college. Valuable information can be given to the students, such as the registration process, applying for financial aid, and the numerous services available to help a student succeed. Naturally, to accommodate different learning styles the online and in-person orientation should be presented visually and auditorily, and use closed caption for online or by voice.

An important feature of orientation, especially on-campus versions, is it brings students together in a relaxed atmosphere to help begin the bonding process to the college and fellow students. It starts to acculturate students into the college. It also acquaints students with administrative rules and regulations, and in some instances it helps students select and design academic programs and find information they need. Most on-campus orientations are led by students who are in their second year. They usually go through a selection and training process and know the ins and outs of life on campus.

A family orientation should be included, which can help family members understand what their son/daughter will experience in the college. This can be particularly important for first-generation college students and their parents. Many parents, especially those of first-generation college students, have no idea the differences between the high school experience and the college experience.

If a student is to commute to the college, family members must become aware of the different requirements and expectations that will be placed on their son or daughter. They will learn that classes begin at various times and to not expect their son or daughter to leave the house at 8 a.m. and return at 3 p.m. as they did in high school.

If their son or daughter is to live in a residence hall, they will learn the expectation of that type of living arrangement. They will meet their son's or daughter's roommate and learn about food services and activities that will take place in each residence hall. Parents will get to see the campus and learn how their son or daughter will be kept safe.

This, again, can occur face to face or over the web. If over the web, the son or daughter will probably have to sit with their parents while using the computer for over-the-web orientation. This is a good thing since the family will be learning about the college experience together and possibly receive a computer lesson.

So, what can colleges do to facilitate orientation? Faculty and staff can serve as mentors and work side by side with student orientation leaders. Also, orientation should be an ongoing process; it should not stop with student enrollment and the beginning of classes. Keep it going; why stop after student enrollment? Get the most benefit out of the student-to-student experience.

Orientation groups should meet at least once per term (face to face or through social media) continuously all years a student is in college. Orientation leaders should keep in touch with their orientation groups. Think about it. A second-year student mentors a first-year student. They all move up each year, so now you have a fourth-year student mentoring a third-year student, a third-year student mentoring the second-year student, who mentors a first-year student. The bonds that can develop between the various student classes—first year, second year, third year, and fourth year—can be invaluable for student success during college and in the future.

Issues that arise for the first-year student may have already arisen the prior year by the second-year orientation group leader. The advice given by the upper-class person to the lower-class person can really eliminate and help solve student issues. It can also contribute to student growth and development by the upper-class person serving as a role model. Naturally, student orientation leaders would have to be chosen judiciously and trained appropriately. But the time and effort devoted to the training could pay off many times over.

Also remember happy alums give generously to the college. The lasting experience that students have with the college can translate into student giving later and referrals to the college. Satisfied students will be the best ambassadors for college recruitment.

ALUMNI GIVING

Why colleges hit up graduates for money the fall after graduation just does not make sense. Most students have student debt to pay off and need to establish themselves in their chosen career. Therefore, why not send a message to students saying something to the effect, "Congratulations on graduating from our college. You have received a world-class education and are ready to embark on the next phase of your life. We know you are establishing yourself in your career and paying off your student debt. We understand that, and instead of soliciting money from you we want to keep you up to date on college happenings. We will send you quarterly college updates, so you know what changes are occurring at your college. We will invite you to participate in events both sporting and cultural. We want you to stay connected with your college. But be assured we will ask you to help us provide scholarships for our students after your third year after graduation. Naturally, if you want to contribute before a formal solicitation, any amount will be accepted. All monies raised from alumni will be used to fund scholarships to help keep the cost of attendance as low as possible. Please also know that you can use our services such as the Career Center as needed."

Give graduates breathing room to become established in their careers. You may be surprised that donations may increase per student after the graduate is established in her/his career. Develop a special newsletter for these students that is sent to them quarterly. Ask students to keep their contact information up to date. Give them a way to do that. Invite them to campus. Give them discounts on merchandise and events on campus. Engender as much good will as possible.

FINANCIAL AID OFFICE

The Financial Aid Office funnels federal and state money into college coffers. The amount of money they bring into a college would boggle the mind. Not many on campus have any idea the amount or percentage of the college budget that is paid for by financial aid. Financial Aid Offices have stringent reporting obligations to federal and state agencies, all the while dispersing funds to students each term so they can attend college. This is an unbroken cycle with no end.

The Financial Aid Office brings in a lot of revenue to the college under sometimes very difficult circumstances. There are very specific regulations that must be adhered to and deadlines that cannot be extended. Financial aid forms can be complicated, especially for first-time college attendees. Often, Financial Aid Offices are understaffed and overworked. They don't receive sympathy from the college community, and that is too bad.

Ask your Financial Aid Office how much revenue they bring to your college each year. You may be amazed at the amount and the overall percentage of the college's budget that is derived from financial aid. Not only does the Financial Aid Office perform its duties under difficult and time-sensitive circumstances, they walk a delicate tightrope having to say "no" to students' requests for aid.

Oftentimes this is due to incorrect filing of forms by students and not submitting forms by specific time frames set by state and federal regulations. The Financial Aid Office is blamed for late processing of aid by state and federal agencies and must explain to college personnel, parents, and students the reason for the delays or denial of aid. Many students and families will blame the Financial Aid Office for phone and email requests going unanswered or delayed due to understaffing.

The Financial Aid Office assists student's ability to attend college and has many contacts with students during each term. What is often overlooked is the amount of contact the Financial Aid Office has with most students. Prior to enrollment, the Financial Aid Office probably has as much contact with a student as the Admissions Office. But once a student enrolls in a college it is the Financial Aid Office that may have the most contact with students, except for professors and parents through direct contact, mailings, web, telephone, and in person. Yet they are not given much status in the college community.

What can be done to help the Financial Aid Office provide the best possible service to students? Colleges need to acknowledge and support the job the Financial Aid Office and staff perform. The office needs to be staffed appropriately to carry out its function effectively and efficiently. The office needs the latest computer equipment and software. The office also needs funding to attend crucial conferences to keep up to date with federal and state regulations.

Since the Financial Aid Office sends so many forms and messages to students, the college public relations department should help develop the message given students when contacted. How many colleges review and help craft Financial Aid Office emails and letters to students and parents? Although specific deadlines must be met to apply for financial aid and the urgency of the message is important, the message can be positive and reassuring.

Instead of saying, "If you do not submit your financial aid forms by XYZ your financial aid request will be denied," say, "We want to assure you receive the financial aid you are qualified to receive. Please be sure to submit your financial aid forms by XYZ. This will ensure that we will be able to process your financial aid request in a timely manner. If you have any questions you can contact us by telephone or email. We look forward to seeing you as a student this fall." This can be a marketing and retention tool.

CAREER SERVICES

It is the belief of many that career services come at the end of the college career; that is, when a student is about to graduate and is looking for a job. Not so for many reasons. To receive financial aid a student must be in a degree program. Even if a student is uncertain of their career area they must choose one if she or he is to receive financial aid.

Since people change careers many times in their lifetime, it seems we are making students choose programs too early in their college career. Also, students who are undecided about a career area leave college at a much greater rate than students with a defined career goal. It does not mean that a student who has a career goal in mind cannot change her/his mind later in college, it simply means that a student who enrolls in college with no career goal has a much higher likelihood of dropping out.

So, what to do to help a student explore career areas? A college should start the career exploration process early on and do not assume that a student knows what he/she wants to do simply since he/she chose a major. Many students simply choose a major to meet the requirement to apply for financial aid. Once enrolled in a program, if a student is not really interested in the program she or he may change majors, delay graduation, or leave the college.

A college can hold career exploration days on campus. This can help students make an informed choice about what program to pursue. Also, having a career exploration component built into the curriculum can have a positive effect on student career choice. Additionally, have career exploration part of orientation and/or ongoing orientation. Use career exploration software in which a new student is required to complete the career software program and meet with a career specialist to interpret results. Colleges can have speakers talk about their careers to students in the classroom or at an all-college assembly.

Earlier it was suggested that all majors hold career days, have alums talk to students, and more. Being able to provide career services can really help a student focus in on potential initial careers. Also remember there are many subsets within basic careers, and career services can help a student understand those subsets so she or he can prepare for them.

Since people change careers many times in a lifetime; the idea here is to get students to think about the future and get to know their strengths and weaknesses. Also, this helps students understand what she or he will encounter in the real world upon graduation. This also gives an appreciation of how a college degree can open doors in the world of work or enable a student to attend college for an advanced degree.

ACADEMIC AND PERSONAL COUNSELING

Academic and personal counseling is another student service contact point that should be encouraged. Faculty need to be trained and know when to contact the Counseling Services to possibly intervene with a student having academic and/or personal issues. Faculty should not act as personal counselors since for the most part they are not trained to provide those types of interventions.

Rather, faculty can be given a general knowledge of what to look for in student behaviors and can provide information to the Counseling Center for proper interventions quickly. The best that can happen is a student tells a counselor she or he was having a bad week and that they are now on track. The worst case is the need for professional outside-the-college intervention to prevent the individual situation from getting worse.

Academic counseling can help students select appropriate programs and courses commensurate with skills and abilities. Academic counseling can help students through a sometimes confusing administrative process. Academic counselors, if not conducted by faculty, can interact or intercede with faculty on a student's behalf. Most students see faculty as sometimes hard to reach out to for additional assistance.

Academic counseling can help by giving the student techniques to use to reach out to faculty. Students are amazed when a faculty member responds positively to a request for additional explanation and/or clarification of coursework and readings. Faculty for the most part are eager and willing to work with students to help them succeed.

Also, personal counseling can help students overcome personal issues and problems. Personal counselors can refer students to appropriate on- and/or off-campus services. It is important and financially cost effective for colleges to work with community services to help students in need of assistance.

There is no reason to duplicate services available in the local community, such as AA or other programs. Colleges need to work closely with their community counterparts to make sure that services for the community are also available for students and vice versa. Sharing of services can be cost effective.

For those colleges that have residence halls, it is important for resident hall staff to interact with students, particularly the first week of classes. Residence hall staff should visit each room and chat with students. If they see that a student has not fully unpacked or made their area of their room their own, then perhaps they are ready to flee the college. An intervention can help the student overcome any anxiety or issues up front and perhaps help the student feel more comfortable with the college.

Resident hall programming can also play an important part to help a student negotiate a complicated college system, especially in the beginning of a student's academic career. During the first few weeks, specific required resident hall meetings can be held on different topics such as dining hall options and where to find information. Guest speakers from the Financial Aid Office and Career Services can also provide necessary information to students to help ensure a good college start.

LEARNING/CLASSROOM COMMUNITIES

There is research on the value of learning and classroom communities. Most are positive. Learning communities can exist in a residence hall, commuter lounge, or the classroom. Generally, learning communities are mostly confined to residence halls. That is, students with similar interests are placed in the same residence hall or floor with roommates with similar interests.

If the residence hall also houses upper-class persons, these students can be a mentor to the new students in specific areas. Also, many residence hall communities group students together that have the same classes. This lends itself to students helping students and can be a powerful learning tool.

Learning communities can be developed in many other college venues. Mostly students are grouped by interest area, curriculum, or courses. Classroom learning communities can be grouped within the classroom by learning styles and/or major. Outside-of-class learning communities can be grouped by clubs, leisure activities, and sports.

Including commuters into learning communities can be very beneficial. Colleges should provide a commuter lounge that goes beyond comfortable chairs and vending machines. There could be a place to rest or take a nap and take a shower and have lockers to secure belongings. Bulletin boards with college events and curriculum activities can be posted.

There can be weekly activities and discussions that pertain to commuter students. Commuters should not be overlooked by colleges even if they make up a small portion of the student population. The community college should particularly take advantage of commuter lounges and activities since most community college students are commuters.

However, wherever learning communities are developed and grouped there should be a mechanism to keeping the communities ongoing. This can be regular learning group meetings and contributing to a social change initiative in the college and/or community. Of course, the social change initiative would coincide with the learning community's interests. Communications can be utilized by the learning communities to include email, social media, web-based classroom discussions, and meeting in various campus areas such as the cafeteria and/or learning resource center.

SOCIAL CHANGE PROJECTS

If colleges are trying to develop good "citizens," then they should have students perform a community service prior to graduation. This can be built in as a culminating credit-bearing course or part of one of the last courses a student takes during the students' last term. Students can work with various faculty with similar interests and develop a plan to carry out a social change project. A written social change paper could be required to pass this requirement.

Students can choose their own projects (and can work in groups), which will benefit the community in which they live either near the campus or where they reside or the college environment. Students need not develop a unique project, which is fine, but they can work with community agencies for their community service projects, such as the Red Cross and other organizations.

The goodwill this would engender would be invaluable to the student, college, or community in which she or he carried out the project. It could also establish lifelong bonds with the student and community and the project selected. Not all projects will come to a positive conclusion, and that is fine as long as the student understands what happened and possible solutions going forward.

HOUSING

The competition is on to which college can offer the most luxurious housing accommodations to students. Colleges feel as if they can lure students to apply and enroll if their campus residence halls impress. On the one hand, this may be true to get a student in the door, but student academic ability to complete courses and programs are the key to student success.

It is true that colleges need to provide suitable housing for their students, both on and off campus. On-campus housing should provide the student with a comfort level that simulates the home environment. That is, comfortable living arrangements, high-speed internet, activities between residence halls, and living-learning communities, among others. Residence hall directors should have highly trained staff that will assist to make the residence hall experience memorable for students.

Off-campus housing is very important too. Living off campus gives a student a sense of real independence. Some colleges maintain off-campus apartment living and inspect housing offered by the public to make sure that minimum student needs are available and met.

Residence life staff should ensure a safe and lasting positive experience for students. Providing enough weekend events for students who live on campus is essential. Residence staff should also take responsibility to try to enhance the experience for those living off campus as well and try to integrate their activities into those who reside on campus.

COMMUTER SERVICES

Even at residential colleges there are commuters. Many four-year colleges are regional and local in nature and cater to commuters, while most community colleges are commuter campuses. Although the academics are the prime reason to attend college and is the primary focus of student retention, the social aspect should not be ignored.

It is true that some ethnic groups emphasize home life and prefer to live at home while attending college. Others live at home and commute to college out of necessity. These students may not be able to afford to go away to college or afford residence hall room and board prices. They also may need to work while attending college to pay tuition.

For the commuter student, colleges need to provide programs and services to help them cope with the lack of interconnection between the college during course attendance and afterward. Often there will be a gap between classes, and although we would like to think that a student would spend that time studying, it is not always the case. Therefore, colleges should provide a comfortable place where commuter students can hang out while waiting for classes.

Commuter lounges can include comfortable seating, game rooms, a study area, and food service, although some will take advantage of campus food services that can be offered at a discount. It would also be nice to provide lockers, a nap area, and a shower for those who come to college directly from work or other activities. Commuter students need to be valued and appreciated, and money should be spent to provide for their comfort and well-being.

STUDENTS WITH SPECIAL NEEDS

College budgets are tight. Federal and state money has shrunk while programs and services for special groups of students have been mandated. Providing services for students with special needs to enable these students to attend college and become independent is long overdue and what we as a society should demand and provide.

However, since colleges are strapped for money, the cost for service personnel such as interpreters and aides are very costly. Students with special needs should not have to compete for resources to help them succeed in college. Colleges both private and public need to recommit themselves to students with special needs and advocate for whatever money it takes to educate this group of students through the federal and state governments. Raising funds through donations and funding campaigns is also a way of providing funding for this group of students with special needs.

BRIDGE PROGRAMS FOR SPECIAL POPULATIONS

Many colleges have established preenrollment programs for special populations of students. These special student populations include minorities at majority institutions, first-generation college students, and those that do not meet the admission criteria but show promise, just to name a few. Colleges that have these programs want to diversify their student bodies and provide the opportunity for students not qualified for acceptance initially to enroll and become successful. Oftentimes this is part of the college mission, and that is a good thing.

Most of these programs provide preenrollment support services such as enhancement of writing and reading skills. They usually meet during the summer months prior to orientation programs. Navigation of the complex college system can also be included with these programs. Students usually live together and participate in academic and social activities as a group. There is much research on these types of programs, and most are positive in their outcomes.

Many of these programs stop once the term begins. It would be best to keep these students together or at least meet as a group once per term to discuss progress and to deal with any issues that may arise. Mentors can be assigned to small groups. It does not seem proper to first provide preenrollment services and then leave these special-situation students on their own after enrollment. Some colleges keep the momentum going throughout the first term or year, but most do not throughout these students' whole college career.

Key ideas of this chapter included the discussion of other programs and services that can assist students to persist. These included: academic and student services, orientation programs, alumni giving, Financial Aid Office, career services, academic and personal services, learning/classroom communities, social change projects, housing, commuter services, students with special needs, and bridge programs for special populations.

Chapter Seventeen

Other Thoughts

While discussing the current educational system and what can be done to help students achieve their academic and personal goals, some other thoughts come to mind about what colleges can do to help students succeed. The blame for unprepared college students flows from the top down. Colleges blame the high schools for not providing rigorous academic programs for students. High schools blame the middle schools who blame the elementary schools who blame parents and society in general. This blame game needs to stop.

There has always been talk about the K–12 educational system and how it does not prepare many of their students for higher education. Some issues include: lack of academic preparation, lack of family with college education, initial enthusiasm displayed by recruitment process but subsequent disappointment once enrolled, and financial need.

So, what can be done? Colleges can adopt a school district. As part of a college faculty teaching load, colleges can provide teachers to teach advanced courses since many districts cannot afford the money for those types of courses. Currently some colleges are partnering with high schools to provide this service, and this is good.

If a faculty member's teaching load is four courses a term, they can teach three on-campus courses, over the web or whatever the current format for teaching is at the college, and teach one course to high school students. These courses do not have to be for college credit but rather advanced courses to help prepare students for the academic rigors of college.

An example of how a college can help educate high school students is the teacher's college example. Years ago, some teacher's colleges had demonstration schools. These schools enrolled a number of students, and classes were taught by college professors. Education students would observe the teaching techniques of their professors.

Another model is to teach one course overload at the high school. The professor would teach the normal teaching load at the college and then teach an additional course at the high school. The college and school district can share the cost of the overload course for the professor. Again, the college would be providing teachers for courses that the high school could not afford to teach and would widen course offerings.

Many may say that this cannot be done due to school district and faculty union concerns. However, this can be overcome easily since everyone's goals is to provide the best education for students and prepare them for further educational opportunities. There are always reasons given why this cannot occur; it is time to figure out how it can occur.

If a college has an education program, this is an ideal way to immerse students into the teaching profession early on as mentors. College students can be mentors in their area of study. Or they can provide mentors in student specific-interest areas such as biology, mathematics, and others. This endeavor can be made a part of the first-year education teaching curriculum to work with an adapted school district from K–12. This could provide teacher education students early on with exposure to teaching.

Students can also visit families at home and invite them to campus as a guest at a cultural and/or sporting event. Most families have not been invited or visited the local college campus for any event. Inviting families, children and parents, and grandparents can really cement the relationship with the college student, college, and K–12 student and parents. Adopting a school system should commence at the earliest time possible, including kindergarten.

Finally, provide aid to promising students so they can attend your college. Those K–12 school district students who go through the college district collaboration can be guaranteed a specific scholarship to attend the local college. This could be a win-win situation for the school district who gets teachers and students to help provide education to its students. This is a winning situation for the college, which has a training area for potential teachers and recruitment of students to the college.

RETHINKING HIGHER EDUCATION

Have you ever wondered why to earn a bachelor's degree it takes four years taking a specific number of courses in sequence? If you have not, maybe you should. There is a move to compress degrees from a four-year to a three-year time period. There is also a move to accept previous work experience for college credit. None of these are new ideas.

The thesis of this book was to show how students need the necessary skills to be successful in foundational courses and beyond. The skill areas can include reading, writing, creative writing, and mathematical skills. But what about a whole curriculum; currently a student takes a specific amount of credit to earn a degree in a specific discipline or major. Many courses overlap or build upon each other, which is good. But many repeat what the student already knows. What can be done?

Why not break a discipline, major, or curriculum into its skill parts? What are the skills needed for a student to be an accountant, liberal arts major, or to earn a psychology degree? Can there be knowledge areas included in the skills area, such as the knowledge of Skinner's theories? Yes, of course. So, can certain disciplines and/or programs be broken into its component skill parts? For most disciplines and programs, they can.

For instance, and an example only not knowing the curriculum or program, let us say to be an accountant 125 different skills and concepts need to be mastered. When a student enters a college or university, what skills in their area of interest does the student already have: 5, 15, 25? If a student possesses 25 of the necessary 125 skills, why should the student need to start at skill one to earn a degree in their area of interest? Why not give the student the skills she or he needs? Perhaps it will take a student two-and-a-half years to earn the skills or five. Does it matter?

Can the skills be delivered in modules, as was explained earlier? Can a student through an internship learn skills by doing? A college once insisted that a graduate student had to enroll full time for two terms to learn to be an administrator. Yet the graduate student was already employed in the field as an administrator. When asked the credentials of the professor teaching the administration course, it was revealed by the professor that he was never an administrator but had read the literature on the subject. You can be the judge of the merits of this encounter that actually took place.

Did the student have to attend two terms full time and take the courses in the area he already knew? Yes. Sometimes our bureaucracies get the better of us, and we just do not do what is in the best interest of the student and college. Sometimes logic does not prevail.

The key idea of this chapter was to discuss alternatives to the current educational system for students completing a certain amount of credits versus knowing specific skills. That is, breaking a degree into skills and assessing students for those missing skills, teach them in modules, and when complete issue a diploma.

Concluding Remarks

This book is to provide colleges a blueprint they can use to actually retain and graduate the students they accept to their institutions. The challenge is for a college to actually evaluate its own courses and processes and to adopt those outlined earlier. It will take an effort on the part of the administration in partnership with faculty staff and students to make this process work. Will it be worthwhile? I think so.

It is not necessary for colleges to expend large sums of money to learn what they already know about their students. The information is already available in their own databases and only needs to be extracted. What colleges do not have is the reading level of the textbooks in their foundation and other classes and the actual skills a student needs to be successful in a course. I contend that getting this information is quite simple. Finding assessment tools to measure student skill levels commensurate with college expectations is also easy.

Developing modules with skill courses to enhance student readiness for college-level courses is also a simple task. Monitoring the system electronically should enable colleges to put their money into these services upfront. Linking classes and programs is also necessary to ensure that a curriculum and/or program mesh together. A top-down review of all programs should be the norm. They are conducted now, but what is left out is the readability of the textbook, skills necessary to be successful, and the linking of courses to a whole curriculum.

It is easy for colleges to blame high schools for lack of student preparation and readiness to attend college. That does not absolve colleges who accept a student to their institution from providing programs and services to help students succeed both academically and personally. The pressure for colleges to retain and graduate students is great. It is my firm belief that implementing the Seidman formula and model will enhance college student retention and especially help students obtain their academic and personal goals. Additionally, implementation of the Seidman formula and model will help colleges achieve their missions of providing a quality education and job preparation for all of their students.

References

ACT. (2017). Institutional Data Files. Retrieved from http://www.act.org/content/dam/act/unsecured/documents/2015-Summary-Tables.pdf.

Almanac of Higher Education 2016–2017 (August 19, 2016). *The Chronicle of Higher Education*, LXII(43).

Astin, A. W. (1993). *What Matters in College? Four Critical Years Revisited.* San Francisco: Jossey-Bass.

College Board. (2016). Education Pays 2016.

Ginder, S. A., J. E. Kelly-Reid, and F. B. Mann. (2015). Graduation Rates for Selected Cohorts 2006–2011; Student Financial Aid, Academic Year 2013–2014; and Admissions in Postsecondary Institutions, Fall 2014: First Look (Provisional Data) (NCES 2015-181). U.S. Department of Education. Washington, DC: National Center for Education Statistics. Retrieved March 12, 2018, from http://nces.ed.gov/pubsearch.

Hoover, E. (February 24, 2006). "Study Finds School-College 'Disconnect' in Curriculum." *Chronicle of Higher Education* 52, no. 25: 1, 37.

Musu-Gillette, L., J. Robinson, J. McFarland, A. KewalRamani, A. Zhang, and S. Wilkinson-Flicker. (August 2016). *Status and Trends in the Education of Racial and Ethnic Groups 2016* (NCES 2016-007). U.S. Department of Education, National Center for Education Statistics. Washington, DC.

Saenz, V. B., S. Hurtado, D. Barrera, D. Wolf, and F. Yeung. (2007). "First in My Family: A Profile of First-Generation College Students at Four-Year Institutions since 1971." Los Angeles: Higher Education Research Institute, UCLA.

Seidman, A. (August 2003). I*t Takes a College Community to Improve Retention and Graduation Rates.* Livingston College [PowerPoint slides]. Copy available from author.

Seidman, A. (ed.) (2005). *College Student Retention: Formula for Student Success.* Westport, CT: ACE/Praeger.

Seidman, A. (2005). "Minority Student Retention: Resources for Practitioners." In *Minority Retention: What Works?* ed. G. H. Gaither, 7–24. San Francisco, CA: Jossey-Bass.

Seidman, A. (ed.) (2012). *College Student Retention: Formula for Student Success*, second ed. New York: ACE/Rowman & Littlefield.

Seidman, A. (2012). "Taking Action: A Retention Formula and Model for Student Success." In A. Seidman (ed.), *College Student Retention: Formula for Student Success*, second ed. New York: ACE/Rowman & Littlefield.

Seidman, A. (June 2017). *Crossing the Finish Line: Retaining and Graduating Your Students*. NASPA Assessment & Persistence Conference, Orlando, FL [PowerPoint slides]. Copy available from author.

Shapiro, D., A. Dundar, F. Huie, P. Wakhungu, X. Yuan, A. Nathan, and Y. A. Hwang. (2017, April). A National View of Student Attainment Rates by Race and Ethnicity—Fall 2010 Cohort (Signature Report No. 12b). Herndon, VA: National Student Clearinghouse Research Center.

Silverman, L., and A. Seidman. (2011–2012). "Academic Progress in Developmental Math Courses: A Comparative Study of Student Retention." *Journal of College Student Retention: Research, Theory & Practice* 13, no. 3: 267–87.

Tinto, V. (1993). *Leaving College: Rethinking the Causes and Cures of Student Attrition*, second ed. Chicago: The University of Chicago Press.

U.S. Department of Education, National Center for Education Statistics. (2000). 1999–2000 National Postsecondary Student Aid Study.

Index

111

About the Author

Dr. Alan Seidman is professor emeritus at Walden University. He is also the executive director of the Center for the Study of College Student Retention (www.cscsr.org). The Center provides retention resources to individuals and educational institutions, including the *Journal of College Student Retention: Research, Theory & Practice*, a Sage publication which Dr. Seidman founded and edits. It is the only scholarly journal devoted exclusively to college student retention issues.

Dr. Seidman's book, *College Student Retention: Formula for Student Success*, second edition, was published in 2012. His book chapter, "Minority Student Retention: Resources for Practitioners" in *Minority Retention: What Works?* was published in 2005, while his second book, *Minority Student Retention: The Best of the* Journal of College Student Retention: Research, Theory & Practice was published in 2007.

Dr. Seidman has also published articles in scholarly journals in the area of retention and attrition, student services, and enrollment management and has given presentations on these topics at local, state, regional, national, and international conferences and presentations/workshops to college and university administrators, faculty, and staff. Dr. Seidman appeared on Fox News Live Weekend to talk about college student retention.

As professor emeritus at Walden University, he has taught doctoral-level courses, served as a specialization coordinator, dissertation chair, and second committee member and served on numerous committees. Dr. Seidman has also been a residency faculty member and is a mentor to a number of students.

In addition to his professional responsibilities, Dr. Seidman is a member of the NH Judicial Council, appointed by the governor of NH and confirmed by the executive council; was appointed by the U.S. Secretary of Commerce as an examiner, Malcolm Baldrige National Quality Award (MBNQA) program; served as the NH alternate to the Taxpayers Advocacy Panel, IRS, U.S. Department of the Treasury; has been a grant reader for the U.S. Department of Education (Upward Bound Grants, Student Support Service Grants, Ronald E. McNair Postbaccalaureate Achievement Program Grants); has been an instructor trainer, American Red Cross; and AARP Volunteer Income Tax Assistance program volunteer.

Dr. Seidman is the recipient of the Walden University Richard W. Riley College of Education & Leadership Extraordinary Faculty award and the State University of New York (SUNY) Chancellor's Award for Excellence in Professional Service.